THE SIXTH SENSE

Also by Mitch Horowitz

Practical Magick
Modern Occultism
Occult America
One Simple Idea
The Miracle Club
Uncertain Places
Daydream Believer
The Seeker's Guide to the Secret Teachings of All Ages
The Miracle Habits
The Miracle Month
Secrets of Self-Mastery
The Miracle of a Definite Chief Aim
The Power of the Master Mind
Magician of the Beautiful
Mind As Builder
Cosmic Habit Force
Happy Warriors

The Napoleon Hill Success Course Series™

The Miracle of a Definite Chief Aim
The Power of the Master Mind
Secrets of Self-Mastery
Going the Extra Mile (by Judith Williamson)
The Sixth Sense

THE NAPOLEON HILL SUCCESS COURSE™

THE SIXTH SENSE

NAPOLEON HILL'S ULTIMATE STEP TO SUCCESS

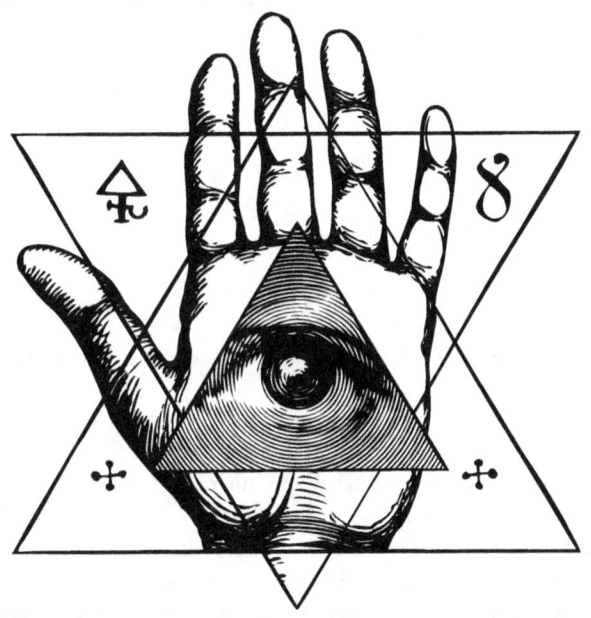

MITCH HOROWITZ

AN APPROVED PUBLICATION OF **THE NAPOLEON HILL FOUNDATION**

Published 2025 by Gildan Media LLC
aka G&D Media
www.GandDmedia.com

THE SIXTH SENSE. Copyright © 2025 The Napoleon Hill Foundation. All rights reserved.

No part of this book may be used, reproduced or transmitted in any manner whatsoever, by any means (electronic, photocopying, recording, or otherwise), without the prior written permission of the author, except in the case of brief quotations embodied in critical articles and reviews. No liability is assumed with respect to the use of the information contained within. Although every precaution has been taken, the author and publisher assume no liability for errors or omissions. Neither is any liability assumed for damages resulting from the use of the information contained herein.

Front cover design by David Rheinhardt of Pyrographx

Interior design by Meghan Day Healey of Story Horse, LLC.

Library of Congress Cataloging-in-Publication Data is available upon request

ISBN: 978-1-7225-0678-0

10 9 8 7 6 5 4 3 2 1

*To the Castel family,
to whom these ideas come naturally.*

Contents

CHAPTER ONE
Empire Of Mind... 9

CHAPTER TWO
Mind Alchemy 21

CHAPTER THREE
Napoleon Hill's Greatest Method....................... 43

CHAPTER FOUR
The Power of a Single Wish 55

CHAPTER FIVE
Escape Predatory Personalities 81

CHAPTER SIX
Why "Never Give Up" Is a Metaphysical Law........... 97

CHAPTER SEVEN
Your Plus-Self 125

CHAPTER EIGHT
The Metaphysics of "Making It"....................... 131

CHAPTER NINE
The Gospel of Carnegie.................................153

CHAPTER TEN
The World Is As You Are..............................157

CHAPTER ELEVEN
It Is Not Too Late......................................165

EPILOGUE
Napoleon Hill's "Secret" 169

APPENDIX A
Psychic Spies to the Rescue? 173

APPENDIX B
Wild Talents: Why ESP Is Real 179

APPENDIX C
The 30-Day Mental Challenge.....................207

INDEX 211
ABOUT THE AUTHOR.............................225

CHAPTER ONE

Empire of Mind

Before starting this book, I attended the show of a mentalist, a stage magician who performs as a psychic. "I will perform the illusion of a 'sixth sense,'" she announced—and did a good job of it. But the message was clear: a sixth sense is the stuff of fantasy.

The premise of this book is the exact opposite.

When Napoleon Hill published *Think and Grow Rich* in 1937 he wrote, rightly, that the functions of the psyche, which I consider a compact of thought and emotion, encompass not just cognition and motor skill but what pioneering parapsychologist J.B. Rhine (1895–1980), who also appears in Hill's landmark, termed extrasensory perception or ESP.

In *Think and Grow Rich*, Hill quotes admiringly from a November 26, 1936, *New York Times* editorial, "What Is 'Telepathy'?": "The actual existence of telepathy and clairvoyance now seems to some scientists enormously probable as the result of Rhine's experiments." Counterclaims soon followed. Perhaps the most colorful appeared in an article of October 19, 1949, "Prof. Rhine of Duke Assailed by Russians," in which "three leading Soviet pedagogues" accused Rhine "and other 'reactionary philosophers'" of "seeking to forestall or postpone the inevitable collapse of capitalism by poisoning the minds of workers" with fantasies of mystical abilities. This critique endures today with modified language.

As is commonly known in our era, telepathy, clairvoyance, and ESP refer to the individual's capacity to glean or convey information in a manner not understood within our current sensory framework—but, as I maintain, in no sense of violative of either Einsteinian or quantum physics, a point demonstrated in replicated laboratory data from academic and independent research facilities and widely discussed conceptual models in theoretical physics.

What I just wrote evokes enduring pushback. So much so that when I ventured similar ideas in 2017 in the first volume of the Napoleon Hill Success Course, *The Miracle of a Definite Chief Aim*, the segment was red-flagged and disputed during the editing process. I was told that while psi phenomena may have seemed promising in 1937 it was since discredited.

As is often the case with rejection of anomalous cognition, opposition rests more on sentiment than science. But science proves resilient. Recent to this writing, for example, a team of social scientists endeavored to evaluate the CIA's famous remote-viewing or psychic-spying program, which ran from about 1972 to 1995 as Project Stargate. In 2023, researchers concluded in the journal *Brain and Behavior* that the chief thrust of the program, whose data was "progressively declassified" between 1995 and 2003, proved empirically sound: "In the case of RV [remote viewing], experiments with significant results greatly predominate."* (See Appendix A: "Psychic Spies to the Rescue?") This has proven so again and again since parapsychology began as a

---

* "Follow-up on the U.S. Central Intelligence Agency's (CIA) remote viewing experiments" by Álex Escolà-Gascón, et al., *Brain and Behavior*, May 3, 2023

formal academic science nearly a century ago thanks in large measure to Rhine's efforts.

The passage that caused controversy in 2017—and bears direct relevance to our explorations in this book—reappears here:

Frontiers of Thought

Have you noticed that when something is impressed upon your mind—such as a deeply held conviction, an intense yearning, or a sense of forward-looking confidence (or the opposites of any of these things), you tend to discover connections, examples, and possibilities that seem to draw you closer to what you are focused on?

It is theoretically possible that one of the reasons a focused thought brings you in proximity to related conditions and people is not simply that you are more aware of relevant circumstances, or are willfully seizing upon confirmations of a pre-determined idea (a phenomenon called "confirmation bias"). Rather, you may be communicating your attitudes in a not yet understood extra-physical fashion to people who may be able to offer assistance, meet you halfway, or provide a necessary piece of information.

Beginning in the early 1930s, Duke University researcher J.B. Rhine conducted hundreds of thousands of trials, eventually spanning decades, in which subjects attempted to "guess" which card was overturned on a five-suit deck consisting of images such as a circle, square, or cross. These were called Zener cards.

Certain individuals made small but statistically relevant "hits" at a higher-than-average rate. Rhine labored intensively, and under the scrutiny of critics, to safeguard against every form of corruption in his data, so much so that his card experiments far exceeded the controls of most clinical trials. These few percentage points of deviation, tracked across years of trials, indicated some form of anomalous transfer of information in a laboratory setting—either that, or the manner in which we compile clinical statistics is flawed in some way that we do not yet understand.

Rhine's lab work has attracted decades of controversy, but his data and research have never been overturned. Napoleon Hill and his key collaborator and benefactor, insurance executive W. Clement Stone, took this topic very seriously, as do I. Warren Weaver, a former president of the American Association for the Advancement of Science, who directed the allocation of hundreds of millions of dollars in medical research grants for the Rockefeller Foundation and Alfred P. Sloan Foundation, examined Rhine's methodology and concluded: "I cannot reject the evidence and I cannot accept the conclusions." Weaver did not share Rhine's views, but as an authentic scientist he refused to close the door on the matter.

I don't want any reader of this book to take my word or Rhine's word that this research is valid. Don't take W. Clement Stone's word—though he thought highly enough of Rhine's work to fund his lab at Duke. Research the topic yourself if it is of interest to you. It would surpass the scope of this book to consider the various implications of Rhine's experiments. For our purposes here, suffice to say: Many thoughtful, seasoned people report remarkable hunches, deeply meaningful coincidences, and fortuitous "accidents," some of which occur in ways that cannot always be defined by ordinary experience or statistical probability.

The mind is an extraordinary frontier. When you are enthusiastically and diligently focused on a desired goal, your mental apparatus sets into motion a remarkable, and not always evident, array of forces.

Popularized though it is, I abide that description. Even as we encounter the nascency of AI and quantum computing, an aspect of the psyche remains glacially unknown, although I venture it is further illuminated by these developments. Your psyche participates, I argue, in a network of events, at once infinite and simultaneous, that occupy different intersections or dimensions of time and occur beyond perceptions of linearity. I will not delay our concerns in this book with extended consideration of psi's verity; I consider the validity of that perspective and evidence for ESP in Appendix B: "Wild Talents," which is a pocket history of psychical research.

While a degree of history and theory necessarily appear in *The Sixth Sense*, the fifth book in the Napoleon Hill Success Course, my effort takes its lead from twentieth-century mystic Neville Goddard (1905–1972) who told students in a 1948 series of lectures in Los Angeles: "Scientists will one day explain why there is a serial universe. But in practice, how you use this serial universe to change the future is more important."

As though responding to Neville's dictum of *pure use*, Google on December 9, 2024, issued this statement about a trial-run of its quantum-computing processor Willow*:

---

* In quantum computing, qubits or quantum bits of data simultaneously exist as 0 and 1 in a state of superposition, enabling radically, almost miraculously, faster computations.

> Willow's performance on this benchmark is astonishing: It performed a computation in under five minutes that would take one of today's fastest supercomputers 10^{25} or 10 septillion years. If you want to write it out, it's 10,000,000,000,000,000,000,000,000 years. This mind-boggling number exceeds known timescales in physics and vastly exceeds the age of the universe. It lends credence to the notion that quantum computation occurs in many parallel universes, in line with the idea that *we live in a multiverse*, a prediction first made by David Deutsch.* [emphasis added]

The worlds of computer engineering and finance, which are exposed to the earliest iterations of quantum computing, are acknowledging theses about our quantum universe more readily and factually than are most philosophical materialists who dominate the social sciences and humanities. It is time for aspiring individuals, including readers of this book, to do the same.

Napoleon Hill proved forward-looking in such matters. This statement from *Think and Grow Rich* conveys the stock he placed in the sixth sense:

> The "thirteenth" principle is known as the SIXTH SENSE, through which Infinite Intelligence may, and

---

* *The Fabric of Reality: The Science of Parallel Universes—and Its Implications* (Viking, 1997). In fairness, it should also be noted that in 1957 physicist Hugh Everett III (1930–1982) postulated the "many-worlds" theory. This is the inceptive model on which Google's statement rests. Everett was attempting to make sense of extraordinary findings documented for about three decades in quantum mechanics. It is likewise noteworthy that Neville's statement preceded Everett's theory by nearly a decade.

will communicate voluntarily, without any effort from, or demands by, the individual.

This principle is the apex of the philosophy. It can be assimilated, understood, and applied ONLY by first mastering the other twelve principles.

The SIXTH SENSE is that portion of the subconscious mind which has been referred to as the Creative Imagination. It has also been referred to as the "receiving set" through which ideas, plans, and thoughts flash into the mind. The "flashes" are sometimes called "hunches" or "inspirations."

Like Hill's books, *The Sixth Sense* is a user's guide. Use benefits from *warranted belief*. The researchers quoted earlier from *Brain and Behavior* note a correlation between results and advocacy in statistical studies of anomalous cognition: "A curious trend and one that should be considered in this context are *sheep-goat* effects. In this effect, individuals who are advocates of parapsychology and who have had psi experiences tend to get a higher number of hits than non-psi experiencers... the distinction between believers and nonbelievers is supported by evidence and is appropriate to apply." As explored in this and other papers, in matters of ESP, belief heightens occurrence. This holds true in medical trials, as proven via the placebo response.*

This contemporary insight supports an earlier observation by American philosopher William James (1842–1910) in his 1895 essay "Is Life Worth Living?": "I confess that I do not see why the

---

* "Altered Placebo and Drug Labeling Changes the Outcome of Episodic Migraine Attacks" by Slavenka Kam-Hansen, et al, *Science Translational Medicine*, January 8, 2014, Vol. 6, Issue 218.

very existence of an invisible world may not in part depend on the personal response which any one of us may make to the religious appeal. God himself, in short, may draw vital strength and increase of very being from our fidelity."

Although these statements reflect different language, eras, and concerns, both reach the same conclusion: *belief abets effect*, not only in terms of perception—though perception, measurement, and matter are demonstrably entangled—but in fact.

The link between hopeful expectancy and heighted effectiveness was similarly bridged by Rhine and his colleagues. The researchers ventured direct connection between mood and test results derived from his Zener card tests for ESP at Duke University's Parapsychology Laboratory in the early 1930s. In the appendix to a British edition of his 1934 monograph *Extrasensory Perception*, Rhine observed in his usual understated manner:

> Since my greatest interest is in stimulating others to repeat some of these experiments, I should like to mention here what has seemed to me to be the most important condition for ESP. This is a spontaneity of interest in doing it. The fresh interest in the act itself, like that of a child in playing a new game, seems to me the most favorable circumstance. Add now... the freedom from distraction, the absence of disturbing skepticism, the feeling of confidence or, at least, of some hope, and I think many good subjects can be found in any community or circle.

In his 1937 *New Frontiers of the Mind*, published the same year as *Think and Grow Rich*, Rhine further emphasized the role of spontaneity, confidence, comity, novelty, curiosity, and lack of fatigue. (And, as it happens, caffeine.)

Following his study of Rhine's trials, psychologist Carl Jung (1875–1961) in his 1952 *Synchronicity* likewise noted the role of enthusiasm in a thought system: "Lack of interest and boredom are negative factors; enthusiasm, positive expectation, hope, and belief in the possibility of ESP make for good results and seem to be the real conditions which determine whether there are going to be any results at all."

Hence, *validated* belief in psychical abilities is in itself a factor heightening results and experiences. This suggests the bridge, however delicate, between parapsychology and the mind-power methods explored in this book. In both categories, passion is critical. Stakes must exist and strong emotions must be in play.

Hidden Tendrils

One last note, which I believe supports the activity of this book. In early adolescence, some of my happiest reading experiences were pulp-era 1930s and 40s novels featuring Doc Savage, a proto-superhero and crusader for justice who recited a variant of French mind theorist Émile Coué's (1857–1926) famous mantra: "Day by day, in every way, I am getting better and better." Doc vowed: "Let me strive every moment of my life to make myself better and better..."

Decades later in 2014, having long since left behind Doc and his team of happy warriors, I first wrote about Coué, who appears in the next chapter, in my *One Simple Idea*, a history of the positive-mind movement. Early drafts of my book proposal titled the work *Empire of Mind*. I later settled on the published title and wrote no more about it.

In 2025, an appreciative reader and brilliant graphic artist, Scorpio Steele, sent me a gift that can only be described as time-bending. Scorpio's colored pencil / marker original work (which I treasure) depicted me as Doc Savage in a pitch-perfect echo, including stylized typeface, of the Doc paperbacks I loved in the late 1970s. His title? *The Empire of Mind*. Front and back appear here.

On the cover, I am flanked by two of my heroes, one already quoted, Neville Goddard, and the other spiritual adventurer and world-traveler Madame H.P. Blavatsky (1831–1891), who Scorpio

uses, among others, as my etheric guides—or, as Napoleon Hill termed it, "Invisible Counselors." The story behind Scorpio's visionary and artistically virtuosic gift demonstrates, for me at least, that tendrils of psyche run deep and multi-directionally—a principle to which we now turn.

To prepare for our journey, say it with me: *Let me strive every moment of my life to make myself better and better . . .*

CHAPTER TWO

Mind Alchemy

"The vibrations of fear," Napoleon Hill wrote in *Think and Grow Rich*, "pass from one mind to another just as quickly and as surely as the sound of the human voice passes from the broadcasting station to the receiving set of a radio—and BY THE SELF-SAME MEDIUM."

But we are not at the mercy—at least not entirely—of fearful or negative psychical states announcing themselves to others. We possess a mechanism that fosters a kind of mind alchemy, altering our dominant thoughts and, in some measure, our moods and self-image. It is called autosuggestion.

"Autosuggestion," Hill wrote, "is self-suggestion. It is the agency of communication between that part of the mind where conscious thought takes place, and that which serves as the seat of action for the subconscious mind."

He continued, "Through the dominating thoughts which one *permits* to remain in the conscious mind, (whether these thoughts be negative or positive, is immaterial), the principle of auto-suggestion voluntarily reaches the subconscious mind and influences it with these thoughts."

In this chapter, I historically and practically explore two dynamic and pioneering techniques of autosuggestion, one devised by early twentieth-century French mind theorist Émile Coué (1857–1926), whom we just met, and the other by mid-century American cosmetic surgeon Maxwell Maltz (1899–1975). Neither, in my estimate, has been surpassed. Both programs are ardently secular or aspiritual; but both serve as tonic to the situation Hill identified: tendency of your psyche to convey its state, whether certain and capable or fearful and doubting, to others around you. I open with Coué.

Day by Day

The name Émile Coué, although one of the most quietly significant in modern placebo studies and motivational philosophy, invites blank looks from most people today. Yet Coué, who earned both adulation and jeers during his lifetime, devised a simple, mantra-based method of self-reprogramming which is indirectly validated across a wide range of disciplines, often by researchers unaware of the inceptive insights upon which their studies rest. I believe that Coué's approach not only deserves new credit and respect, but holds promise for anyone seeking practical methods of autosuggestion and improvement of self-image.

Coué prescribed mantras or affirmations to reprogram your psyche along lines of confidence, enthusiasm, and vitality. His methods prefigured the work of self-help icons like Hill, Anthony Robbins, and Maxwell Maltz, whom we next meet, as well as recent clinical developments in sleep, neurological, placebo, and psychical research.

At one time, thousands of people in the U.S. and Europe swore by Coué's approach. His key mantra—"Day by day, in every way, I am getting better and better"—was repeated by the Beatles, along with a wide range of therapists and spiritual writers. In rediscovering Coué, you can easily determine for yourself if his basic technique works.

Before exploring Coué's method and its application, it is useful to understand the factors that shaped him. Born in Brittany in 1857, Coué developed an early interest in hypnotism, which he pursued through a mail-order course from Rochester, New York. Coué studied hypnotic methods more rigorously in the late 1880s with French physician and therapist Ambroise-Auguste Liébeault (1823–1904). Liébeault was among the founders of the so-called "Nancy School" of hypnotism, which promoted hypnotism's therapeutic uses. Leaving behind concepts of occultism and cosmic laws, Nancy hypnotists considered their treatment a practical form of suggestion, mental recalibration, relaxation, and psychotherapy.

This was Coué's view, supported by personal experience. While working in the early 1900s as a pharmacist in Troyes, in northwestern France, Coué happened upon a startling discovery: patients responded better to medications when he spoke in praise of the formula. Coué came to believe that the imagination—in this case stirred by hopeful expectancy—aided not only recovery but overall well-being. From this insight, Coué developed his method of "conscious autosuggestion." It was essentially a form of *waking hypnosis* using self-administered, confidence-building mantras in a relaxed or semiconscious state.

Coué argued that many of us suffer from poor self-image. This problem is unconsciously reinforced when our willpower, or drive to achieve and improve, is overcome by our imagination, by which he meant habitual self-perceptions, which are often negative or fearful. In 1922, he wrote in *Self Mastery Through Conscious*

Autosuggestion, "When the will and the imagination are opposed to each other, it is always the imagination which wins."

By way of example, Coué asked audiences to imagine walking across a wooden plank laid on the floor, an easy task for most. But if that same plank is elevated, say, twenty feet off the ground, the task grows fraught with fear (which also makes us more accident prone), even though the physical demand is unchanged. This, Coué argued, is what we are constantly doing on a mental-emotional scale when we imagine ourselves worthless or weak.

These insights drove the autosuggestion founder toward his signature achievement. Coué believed that through self-suggestion, any individual, with nearly any problem, could induce the same positive results he observed when working in Troyes. In pursuit of an overarching method, Coué devised his self-affirming mantra: "Day by day, in every way, I am getting better and better."

Although few today have heard of Coué, many recognize his signature phrase, which he popularized through lecture tours of Europe and the U.S. in the early 1920s. I had the privilege of knowing Jean-Gabriel Castel (1927–2023), a decorated member of the French Resistance and pioneer in international law—and maternal grandfather of my partner, filmmaker Jacqueline Castel—who recited Coué's mantra daily in its original French (*"Tous les jours, à tous points de vue, je vais de mieux en mieux"*).

To critics, however, Coué reflected everything fickle and faddy about affirmative-mind and motivational philosophies. How, they wondered, could anyone believe that this singsong mantra—*Day by day, in every way, I am getting better and better*—could solve anything? But in a facet of Coué's career that is often overlooked, he demonstrated considerable insight—later validated by sleep and placebo researchers—in how he prescribed *using* the formula.

Coué explained that you must recite the "day by day" mantra just as you are drifting to sleep at night, suspended in the exquisitely relaxed state between wakefulness and slumber. Sleep researchers now call these periods *hypnagogia*, an intriguing stage of mind during which you possess sensory awareness but your perceptions of reality bend and morph, like images from a painting by surrealist Salvador Dalí, whom we soon encounter.*

During hypnagogia, your mind is uniquely supple and suggestible. Coué realized this by observation and deemed it the period to gently whisper twenty repetitions: "Day by day, in every way, I am getting better and better." The therapist did not want you to rouse yourself from near-sleep by counting, so he suggested knotting a small string twenty times and using this device like rosary beads to mark off recitations. He instructed repeating the same procedure the instant you wake in the morning, which is sometimes called *hypnopompia* (coined by psi research pioneer F.W.H. Myers). It is similar to the nighttime state insofar as you occupy a netherworld of consciousness, yet in both stages you retain cognition and capacity for mental intention.

Since these states are apparently inviting periods for self-suggestion—the mind is flexible, the body relaxed, and the psyche unclouded by stimuli—Coué taught using this period for his mantra-based routine, which, he argued, reorients your psyche, tones your self-image, and strengthens your abilities. Was he right? There exists one way to know, at least for private purposes: *Try*. We must never place ourselves above what some consider "easy" ideas.

---

* French dream researcher and physician Alfred Maury (1817–1892) coined the term hypnagogia, which was popularized by psychologist Andreas Mavromatis in his like-named 1987 monograph.

In Arthur Conan Doyle's 1892 Sherlock Holmes story "The Adventure of the Copper Beeches," his hero cries: "Data! data! data! I can't make bricks without clay." Here is where you as a seeker gather data.

Once upon a time, someone who did not understand my work asked whether I use the methods in this chapter. I use them like I drink water. The road is long—the results are real.

* * *

My search is influenced by twentieth-century spiritual teacher Jiddu Krishnamurti (1895–1986), who emerged from Theosophical and Vedic tradition but developed into an uncategorizable intellect. Krishnamurti observed that the chief impediment to self-development and independent thought is the wish for *respectability*. Nothing does more to stunt personal experiment, he taught, than following the current of accepted inquiry—which brings rewards of its own, including within subcultures and places of employment. Once you fixate on joining that current, nearly everything you read, hear, or encounter is evaluated on whether it places you within it.

Recent to this writing, I attended a panel at a major art museum in which a speaker made political pronouncements—to some applause, I must concede—that sounded to me like guild rites of fealty: emotionless and loveless but hitting the right notes. There are greater currents to join.

So, if you are unafraid of a little hands-on philosophy (and you must not be if you are reading this chapter), Coué offers the perfect opportunity.

A final word on method. I am sometimes asked: can I devise my own mantra? Of course. I note only that Coué intended his affirmation to cover all purposes and circumstances. I suggest starting with it to grow accustomed to the practice. Thereafter, if you like, remove the training wheels and structure mantras of your own.

Coué's Reach

It may help to realize that Coué's influence traveled in remarkable directions. The Beatles tried Coué's method and apparently liked it, as references to Coué appear in some of their songs. In 1967, Paul McCartney used Coué's mantra in the infectious chorus of "Getting Better," "It's getting better all the time...," and the lyrics paid further tribute to the healer: "You gave me the word, I finally heard / I'm doing the best that I can." John Lennon recited Coué's formula in his 1980 "Beautiful Boy," "Before you go to sleep, say a little prayer: Every day, in every way, it's getting better and better."

Beyond the Fab Four, placebo researchers at Harvard Medical School validated one of Coué's core insights. In January 2014, clinicians from Harvard's program in placebo studies published a paper reporting that migraine sufferers respond better to medication when given "positive information" about the drug.* This was the same observation Coué had made in the early 1900s. Harvard's study is considered a landmark because it suggests that the placebo response is ever operative. It is the first study to use suggestion, in this case accurate news about a drug's efficacy, in connection with an active versus inert substance, and hence establishes, at least as an evidence-backed hypothesis,

---

* "Altered Placebo and Drug Labeling Changes the Outcome of Episodic Migraine Attacks" by Slavenka Kam-Hansen, et al, *Science Translational Medicine*, January 8, 2014, Vol. 6, Issue 218.

that *expectation* impacts how, and to what extent, we experience a drug's effects.

Although the Harvard paper echoes Coué's original insight, it makes no mention of him. I wondered whether researchers had Coué in mind when they designed the study. I asked the primary author who did not respond. So, I contacted the director of Harvard Medical School's program in placebo studies, Ted J. Kaptchuk, a remarkable and inquisitive clinician who also worked on the study. "Of course I know about Coué," Kaptchuk told me, "'I'm getting better day by day.'" He agreed that the migraine study coalesced with Coué's observations, though added the researchers had not been thinking of him when they designed it.

Coué's impact appears below the radar in an unusual range of places. An influential twentieth-century British Methodist minister, Leslie D. Weatherhead (1893–1976), was active in the Oxford Group in the 1930s, which preceded Alcoholics Anonymous (AA) in devising a program of religious-therapeutic recovery. The clergyman sought a way for patients and addicts to therapeutically accept the truth and power of affirmations, especially when such statements contradict circumstantial reality, as in cases of chronically low self-worth. In using suggestions or affirmations to improve self-image and leaven limiting beliefs, Weatherhead was updating Coué's methods.

The minister realized that certain affirmations—such as "I am confident and poised"—could not penetrate the "critical apparatus" of the human mind, which he compared to "a policeman on traffic duty."

Other physicians and therapists likewise noted the problem of affirmations lacking *emotional persuasiveness*. Some therapists observed that affirmations had to be credible to reach a subject; no reasonable person would believe histrionic or exaggerated self-claims, a point Coué also made. While Weatherhead shared these critiques, he believed that the rational "traffic cop" is eluded by two practices. First is the act of repetition: "A policeman on duty who refuses, say, a cyclist the first time, might ultimately let him into the town if he presented himself again and again," he wrote in his 1951 *Psychology, Religion, and Healing*. Continuing the metaphor, Weatherhead took matters further:

> I can imagine that a cyclist approaching a town might more easily elude the vigilance of a policeman if the attempt to do so were made in the half-light of early dawn or the dusk of evening. Here also the parable illumines a truth. The early morning, when we waken, and the evening, just as we drop off to sleep, are the best times for suggestions to be made to the mind.

As Weatherhead grasped, the hypnagogic state—again, the drowsy stage between wakefulness and sleep, generally experienced when you are drifting off in the evening or waking in the morning—poses a period of unique psychological flexibility when ordinary barriers are lowered. This is pure Couéism. Moreover, this fact probably explains why people experiencing depression or anxiety often describe the early waking hours as their toughest time of day: the rational defenses are slackened. What may seem manageable in daylight is fearsome during the twilight of the psyche. But—"Every stick has two ends," as twentieth-century spiritual philosopher G.I. Gurdjieff (1866–1949) noted. If the individual uses the gentlest efforts to repeat affirmations, without rousing himself to a waking state, the new self-conceptions, dropped into a suggestible and vulnerable mind, gradually form roots.

Mystic Neville Goddard (1905–1972) ventured a similar point about the malleability of the hypnagogic mind. So did twentieth-century psychical researcher and scientist Charles Honorton (1946–1992), who used this observation as the basis for telepathy trials between individuals. Honorton considered hypnagogia "prime time" for extrasensory perception or ESP.

In the early 1970s, Honorton and collaborators embarked on a long-running series of telepathy trials called the "ganzfeld" experiments (German for "whole field"). These trials were designed to induce hypnagogia in the "receiver." The subject was placed, seated or reclining, in a soft-lit or darkened room and fitted with eyeshades and earphones to create a state of comfortable sensory deprivation or low-level stimulation (such as with a "white noise" machine). Seated in another room, the "sender" attempted to mentally convey a random, machine-selected image to the receiver. Once the sending period ended, the receiver was asked to identify a correct image from among four—three were decoys, establishing a chance hit-rate of 25 percent. In aggregate, receivers consistently scored above-chance hits on the "sent" image.

Honorton collaborated with avowed skeptic and research psychologist Ray Hyman in reviewing data from a wide range of ganzfeld experiments. The psychical researcher and skeptic jointly wrote: "We agree that there is an overall significant effect in this database that cannot be reasonably explained by selective reporting or multiple analysis."* Honorton added, "Moreover, we agree that the significant outcomes have been produced by a number of different investigators."

---

* "A Joint Communiqué: The Psi Ganzfeld Controversy" by Ray Hyman and Charles Honorton, *Journal of Parapsychology*, vol. 50, December 1986

Hyman insisted that none of this is proof of psi, though he later acknowledged: "Contemporary ganzfeld experiments display methodological and statistical sophistication well above previous parapsychological research. Despite better controls and careful use of statistical inference, the investigators seem to be getting significant results that do not appear to derive from the more obvious flaws of previous research."*

Although psychical research has come under withering, and often unfair criticism in recent years,** the ganzfeld experiments have remained relatively untouched at least in impartial evaluations. Their methodological basis rests on Coué's insights.

It Works

Coué's presence also emerges in popular literature. One of the most enduring and beguiling pieces of mass metaphysics on the American scene is a twenty-eight-page pamphlet called *It Works*, written in 1926 by a Chicago ad executive named Roy Herbert Jarrett, who used the alias *R.H.J.* His widely adopted method is to write down and focus on your desires: first, you must clarify your need; second, write it down and think of it always; and third, tell no one what you are doing to maintain mental steadiness. Plain enough, but the author's insights drawn upon deeper aspects of Couéism.

In early 1923, Coué embarked on a three-week lecture tour of America, making one of his final stops in Jarrett's hometown of Chicago. The Frenchman addressed a packed house at Orches-

---

* "Evaluation of a Program on Anomalous Mental Phenomena" by Ray Hyman, *Journal of Parapsychology*, 1995, Vol. 59, No. 4

** E.g., see my "Question Authorities: How the social sciences pathologize belief in the paranormal," Substack, May 6, 2025.

tra Hall. A raucous crowd of more than 2,000 demanded that the therapist help a paralytic man who had been seated onstage. Coué defiantly told the audience that his autosuggestive treatments worked only on illnesses that originated in the mind. "I have not the magic hand," he insisted. Nonetheless, Coué approached the man and told him to concentrate on his legs and repeat, "It is passing, it is passing." The seated man struggled up, haltingly walked, and the crowd exploded. Coué rejected any notion that his "cure" was miraculous and insisted that the man's disease must have been psychosomatic.*

To some Americans, Coué's message of self-affirmation held particular relevance for dispossessed people. The pages of Black nationalist Marcus Garvey's (1887–1940) newspaper, *Negro World*, echoed Coué's "day by day" mantra in an editorial headline: "Every Day in Every Way We See Drawing Nearer and Nearer the Coming of the Dawn for Black Men." The paper editorialized that Garvey's teachings provide the same "uplifting psychic influence" as Coué's.**

Coué took special liking to Americans. He found American attitudes a refreshing departure from what he experienced back home. "The French mind," he wrote in 1923 in *My Method, Including American Impressions*, "prefers first to discuss and argue on

---

* Coué is quoted in Chicago from "Coué Proves Theory Worth," *Los Angeles Times*, February 7, 1923. (I altered the article's amusing use of the phonetic "ze" for "the" in its attempt to capture his French accent.) Additional articles on Coué's first American tour, which he briefly reprised in 1924, include "Crowd in Orchestra Hall Cheers Coué as His First Attempt in Chicago to Effect Cure Seems a Success," *Chicago Daily Tribune*, February 7, 1923; "Youth's Tremors Quieted by Coué," *New York Times*, January 14, 1923; and "Emile Coué Dead, a Mental Healer," *New York Times*, July 3, 1926.

** The *Negro World* headline appeared September 15, 1923. The editorial quote is from February 10, 1923.

the fundamentals of a principle before inquiring into its practical adaptability to everyday life. The American mind, on the contrary, immediately sees the possibilities of it, and seeks... to carry the idea further even than the author of it may have conceived."

The therapist could have been describing salesman-seeker Roy Herbert Jarrett and many others in American's positive-mind tradition. "A short while ago," Jarrett wrote in 1926, the year of Coué's death, "Dr. Emil [sic] Coué came to this country and showed thousands of people how to help themselves. Thousands of others spoofed at the idea, refused his assistance, and are today where they were before his visit."

Just as Coué observed about the American mind, Jarrett sought to boldly expand the uses of autosuggestion. Sounding the keynote of America's metaphysical tradition, Jarrett believed that subconscious-mind training does more than recondition the psyche: it activates a divine inner power that out-pictures one's mental images into surrounding life. "I call this power 'Emmanuel' (God in us)," Jarrett wrote. In effect, all of American positive-mind culture employs Coué-style methods.

Coué's instincts spoke to the individual's deepest wish for self-help and personal empowerment. In my observation, as both historian and seeker, people across generations have benefited from his ideas. So, once more, I invite you to self-experiment with Coué's method. We all possess the agency of personal experiment; it may be the area in life where we are most free. Yet we get so wrapped up in the lure of digital culture that we overlook the technology of thought, through which we may be able to significantly reform aspects of self, surroundings, and experience.

You may discover that the ideas of this mind pioneer, a figure under-recognized today, offer the simplicity and effectiveness you seek.

Coué Speaks

For a brief but complete explanation of how to use Coué's method, I am providing the words of the visionary himself from his 1922 *Self-Mastery Through Conscious Autosuggestion*:

How to Practice Conscious Autosuggestion

Every morning on awakening and every evening as soon as you are in bed, close your eyes, and without fixing your attention in what you say, pronounce twenty times, just loud enough so that you may hear your own words, the following phrase, using a string with twenty knots in it for counting:

"DAY BY DAY, IN EVERY WAY, I AM GETTING BETTER AND BETTER."

The words: "IN EVERY WAY" being good for anything and everything, it is not necessary to formulate particular autosuggestions.

Make this autosuggestion with faith and confidence, and with the certainty that you are going to obtain what you desire.

Moreover, if during the day or night, you have a physical or mental pain or depression, immediately affirm to yourself that you are not going to CONSCIOUSLY contribute anything to maintain the pain or depression, but that it will disappear quickly. Then isolate yourself as much as possible, close your eyes, and pass your hand across your forehead, if your trouble is mental, or over the aching part of your body if physical, and repeat quickly, moving your lips, the words: "IT PASSES, IT PASSES," etc. Continue this as long as may be necessary, until the mental or physical pain has disappeared, which it usually does within twenty or twenty-five seconds.

Begin again every time you find it necessary to do so. Like the first autosuggestion given above, you must repeat this one also with absolute faith and confidence, but calmly, without effort. Repeat the formula as litanies are repeated in church.

Surgeon as Seeker

One of the most exciting and popular mental reconditioning programs of the 1960s and beyond emerged from the work of a clinician who, like Coué, experienced the simple realization that *self-image is destiny*—and self-image is alterable. He called his method Psycho-Cybernetics.

This trenchantly secular program of self-development and reconditioning was devised in 1960 by a renowned reconstructive surgeon, Maxwell Maltz (1899–1975). Psycho-Cybernetics won the allegiance of a wide-range of professional athletes, as well as cultural figures including actress Jane Fonda, First Lady Nancy Reagan, and surrealist Salvador Dalí. Pop icon Brian Wilson was photographed with a copy of Maltz's book.

Artist Dalí and the surgeon forged a close friendship and even vacationed together. In 1966, the surrealist master created a painting "Darkness and Light" inspired by Psycho-Cybernetics, which he gave Maltz as a gift. It later appeared on the cover of an updated edition of Maltz's like-named bestseller. As an acquisitions editor at Penguin Random House, I had the opportunity to review personal correspondence between the author and artist in the files of Maltz's publisher Prentice-Hall, which the larger press had acquired.

In short, Maltz believed that self-image, above any other single factor, determines the vector of one's life—and *self-image is malleable to individual will*. This, too, is pure Couéism.

His epiphanic moment arrived this way: as a pioneering cosmetic surgeon, Maltz was among the first generation to perfect reconstructive surgical techniques. Educated at Columbia, Maltz began treating patients in the 1920s; they included victims of burns and accidents, and others who suffered deformities or birth defects (real and exaggerated), which impaired daily functioning.

After years of medical practice, Maltz made a startling observation. Most of his patients *did* experience marked improvement in self-image following successful surgeries—yet a small but persistent number *did not*, at which the clinician wondered. Why, he asked, was the low self-image of some patients apparently resistant to an improvement in appearance? And what—really—is this thing we call "self-image?"

Maltz grew convinced that self-image results, to great extent, from unconscious messages and concepts that you internalize and constantly—often unknowingly—repeat to yourself from your earliest age. Such a pattern can prove crippling or uplifting. And it is changeable.

This insight formed the basis of Maltz's 1960 bestseller, a book that retains loyal readership today. In *Psycho-Cybernetics*, Maltz argues that your mind functions according to the self-regulating system of cybernetics, a concept popularized in 1948 by mathematician Norbert Wiener (1894–1964). Cybernetics describes the mechanism behind a heat-seeking missile, which, once programmed, carries out its directive with flawless self-correction.

In a similar sense, you too function, Maltz writes, as a sophisticated, circuit-loop mechanism—yet unlike engineered apparatuses, or even computers, you operate on *self-suggestion*.

Maltz's program for reconditioning is not for the weak-willed or impatient. It is rigorous. In brief, it requires:

1. At least a half-hour daily of deeply relaxed meditation.

2. Another half-hour of self-guided, visualization-based meditation, in which you picture yourself and your life exactly as you want it to be, within the categories of reason. (Canniness and emotional functionality are prerequisites to the program.)

3. A steady, supplemental practice of affirmations, visualizing, and journaling.

Lest this sound easy, consider: everything in our lives—especially in the age of hand-held devices unknown in Maltz's era—conspires to rob us of meditation, self-reflection (versus morbid self-interest), and some modicum of quietude. Have you ever tried meditating for two thirty-minute periods a day? It is more difficult than it sounds, especially if you already have a meditative practice, such as Transcendental Meditation (my personal choice), to which *Psycho-Cybernetics* exercises are added or accommodated.

Does Maltz's program work? Personal experience tells me that it does—but with two caveats:

1. As alluded, the program requires significant self-discipline and inner effort. There is a secret key to every self-help program. It is absolute, ravenous hunger for self-change. Absent that,

self-help is a hobby. It is to personal growth what humming is to music. But with the right degree of hunger, any legitimate program—from the twelve-steps to TM—can make a difference. But never underestimate the depth of passion required to sustain and drive your efforts. As C.S. Lewis wrote in his 1952 *Mere Christianity*: "All depends on really wanting."

2. Maltz died in 1975, before the neurologic and biologic antecedents of our psychology were well understood. I think he underestimated the influence, and mysteries, of temperamental and characterological traits. Every sensitive parent notices that his or her children enter life—from earliest infancy—with pronounced personality markings, which follow them all their lives. My two sons, the elder of whom turned twenty-one as of this writing, evinced temperamental traits from literally the moment they emerged from the womb. I recognize these characteristics in them today. The nature-nurture debate is a circle with no demarcation where one influence ends and another begins. I believe that Maltz, partly due to his generation, overestimated conditioning and failed to consider the impact of intrinsic personality, and how biochemistry may tend one person toward exuberance and another toward depression.

Moreover, I am certain that Maltz, as a cosmetic surgeon, would have acknowledged that general appearance places considerable weight on scales of self-perception.

In any case, all but the most orthodox determinists would agree that conditioning is a seismic force. Seen in a certain light, the fact of innate personality *elevates* conditioning since your conditioned self informs how you *navigate* implacable aspects of character.

Getting the Word Out

Books sometimes take a twist in the road before finding their audience. Prentice-Hall issued *Psycho-Cybernetics* in 1960 and licensed paperback reprint rights that year to enterprising publisher Melvin Powers (1922–2013) at his Wilshire Book Company in Los Angeles. With Powers, the book found its major success. The LA publisher, who also reissued the popular *Three Magic Words* by U.S. Andersen, had an eagle eye for mind-power classics that were neglected or undersold in earlier editions.

Allow me a byroad to explore how metaphysical books sometimes break through. U.S. Andersen was the pen name of Uell Stanley Andersen (1917–1986), a retired pro-football player, novelist, and metaphysical writer. Andersen's *Three Magic Words* first appeared in 1954 under the title *The Key to Power and Personal Peace*, as published by Hermitage House (a New York press that had incidentally issued L. Ron Hubbard's first edition of *Dianetics* four years prior). Andersen's book was republished in 1956 under its current title by Christian press Thomas Nelson & Sons, and later by Powers' Wilshire Book Company. In its retitled version, *Three Magic Words* gained wide popularity. Let it be remembered: titles matter.

Napoleon Hill, who coined one of the best titles in modern history in *Think and Grow Rich*, recounts this story in his signature book:

> A publisher of books, which sell for a nickel, made a discovery that should be worth much to publishers generally. He learned that many people buy titles, and not contents of books. By merely changing the name of

one book that was not moving, his sales on that book jumped upward more than a million copies. The inside of the book was not changed in any way. He merely ripped off the cover bearing the title that did not sell, and put on a new cover with a title that had "box-office" value.

I recognize this truth from long experience. During my publishing days, I commissioned, at generous advance, a series of essays from a successful author who proposed the title *Notes from the End Times*. It was provocative, daring, and brave. The moment he uttered the phrase in my office we locked eyes and laughed: *this is it*. He later insisted on (and I foolishly allowed) a safer and more equivocal title. The book died. Elsewhere in my company a publisher bought a provocatively titled book that the author wished to tone down *after* the deal was signed. She threated to cancel the book if the title changed. She was right. The title stayed—the book sold.

Psycho-Cybernetics effectively set the template for all secular forms of popular self-help and motivational philosophy in the latter twentieth and early twenty-first centuries. If you attend a business-oriented or life-coaching self-help program—one with a non-spiritual tone—chances are you are imbibing material from Maltz.

I harbor special love for Maltz's book and program because it conveys a sense of epic possibility about the potential of the individual to recondition his self-perception, without requiring any belief system at the door. *Psycho-Cybernetics* envisions the individual as capable of attaining greater heights than, say, Cognitive

Behavioral Therapy (CBT), which can seem to simply rearrange the lawn furniture of the mind.

The book's only requirement is zeal to experiment. Different people will, of course, have different results from, and responses to, Maltz's approach. But consider: what more noble undertaking exists than striving to improve your nature and strengthen your sense of self-direction? All of it without sectarian bent or necessary leap of religious faith.

Seen in this light, Maltz's program stands with the most popular expressions of humanist philosophy of the twentieth century. Its message, like Coué's, remains decisive and hopeful today.

CHAPTER THREE

Napoleon Hill's Greatest Method

I have learned many methods from Napoleon Hill. The one that has served me most lastingly and consistently is sex transmutation, a technique that not only heightens effectiveness, acumen, and charisma, but fosters the insights of the sixth sense. Hill wrote in *Think and Grow Rich* in his chapter "The Mystery of Sex Transmutation":

> While on this exalted plane of THOUGHT, the creative faculty of the mind is given freedom for action. The way has been cleared for the sixth sense to function, it becomes receptive to ideas which could not reach the individual under any other circumstances. The "sixth sense" is the faculty which marks the difference between a genius and an ordinary individual.

This chapter explores the truths whispered in his statement—both their basis in history and their use in the here and now.

The harnessing of sexual desire—referenced historically in obfuscatory if elegant language—unites the Old-World alchemist to the contemporary seeker. The sexual urge, properly transmuted, moves you toward a desired end. Within occult history, terms abound that whisper what I describe. Since I consider historical understanding critical to esoteric working, I open with some background—followed by the simplest application I know.

Before I look to the past—and if you are not fascinated with thought history and want only the "goodies," you are in the wrong place—I venture a clarification. There appears in the method I describe, and how I describe it, a quality of attainment or *acquisitiveness*, if I use the term that is toughest on me, as I believe every seeker should. I draw no distinctions in my search between higher and lower iterations of magick.* I would not know where to draw such demarcations, as another's needs or wishes may be decipherable only to self. In any case, in my system no one need qualify aims. At this stage of my search, I consider the purpose of life, and of exploring greater circles of life, *self-expression*, broadly defined.

"Astral Light"

Pioneering nineteenth-century occult revivalist Eliphas Lévi (1810–1875), the nom de mystique of Alphonse-Louis Constant, posited existence of "astral light" as the vital energy behind magickal operations. This comports with near-contemporaneous references to invisible or vital forces such as Edward Bulwer-Lytton's "Vril" in his liked-titled 1871 novel, *Vril: The Power of the Coming Race*; occult healer Franz Anton Mesmer's "animal magnetism;" Aleister Crowley's "True Will;" Austin Osman Spare's

---

* I use Aleister Crowley's spelling of magick, derived from early modern English, to distinguish occult magick from stagecraft. The term magick itself is rooted in the Greek-Persian *magus*, meaning hereditary priest.

"Kia;" and, most significantly, Arthur Schopenhauer's view of imagination in his 1836 *On Will in Nature*: "Man had not learnt to direct *the light of speculative thought* towards the mysterious depths of his own inner self."* (emphasis mine)

In referencing "astral light," Lévi was echoing but not exactly copying Schopenhauer's "light of speculative thought." The occultist metaphorically identified directed or transmuted thought; and yet it was not wholly metaphorical if one considers neurological pathways through which electrical impulses travel in the brain. Lévi, like Mesmer before him, dramatized a force that humanity had not yet come to understand: inner workings of mind and existence of a glacial subconscious or subliminal thought-emotive center, or psyche.

In ways both profoundly affecting and dynamic, Lévi interpreted magickal operations as a means of arousing and enlisting this mysterious force, which he also compared to the "serpent of Genesis." Such a force, Lévi reasoned, could be summoned through the sexual urge and directed via focused imagination.

Here is Lévi from his 1856 *Doctrine and Ritual of High Magic* translated by John Michael Greer and Anthony Mikituk, which I published at Penguin Random House in 2017. (Greer and Mikituk's translation is the first full English rendering of Lévi's work since Arthur Edward Waite's 1896 *Transcendental Magic*; I consider it the flagship edition.)

> The astral light is the universal seducer symbolized by the serpent of Genesis. This subtle agent, always active, always luxuriant with life blood, always embel-

---

* I quote from the 1903 translation by Jessie Hillebrand aka Madame Karl Hillebrand (1827–1905).

lished with seductive dreams and sweet images; this blind force is subordinate to every will, either for good or for evil; this continually reemerging circulus of an uncontrolled life, which causes giddiness in the imprudent; this corporeal spirit, this fiery body, this impalpable and always present ether; this immense seduction of nature, how can it be completely defined and how can its action be qualified? Indifferent, in a way, on its own, it lends itself just as easily to good as to evil; it carries the light and propagates the darkness; we can also call it Lucifer or Lucifuge; it is a serpent, but it is also an aureole; it is a fire, but one that can as easily belong to the torments of hell as to the offerings of incense promised in heaven. To take possession of it, one must, like the predestined woman, place one's feet on its head.

A name of uncertain origin, *Lucifuge* sometimes refers to the prime minister of Satan. In Latin, it is translated as one who flees light. The image of the woman treading on the head of a serpent appears on the Miraculous Medal, revealed in Paris in 1830 to Catherine Labouré. It is a remarkable symbol of layered depth. Those who hate or proffer conspiracy theories about Catholicism do so because it contains aspects of the Universal Religion, if there is such thing, and I believe there is. Again, Lévi:

> Let us declare here without bandying about that the great magical agent, the double current of light, the living and astral fire of the earth was symbolized by the serpent with the head of a bull, of a goat, or a dog in the ancient theogonies. It is the double serpent of the caduceus; it is the ancient serpent of Genesis; but

it is also the brazen serpent of Moses, interlaced with the tau, that is to say the generative lingam; it is also the goat of the Sabbath and the Baphomet of the Templars; it is the Hyle of Gnostics; it is the double tail of the serpent which form the legs of the solar cockerel of Abraxas; finally it is the devil of M. Eudes de Mirville, and it is actually the blind force that souls must conquer to break free of the chains of the Earth... All magical work thus consists of freeing oneself from the coils of the ancient serpent, then placing one's foot on his head and driving him where one wishes.

This force could be termed emotionalized thought, sexually charged thought, willpower, psyche, or, as I see it, all these. Lévi believed that the ancient symbols—Tarot (in his reading), alchemical sigils, the pentagram, the serpent, Baphomet, the parabolic myths and ancient fables—were at once reflections of and methods toward arousing awareness and use of this elemental force: sexuality-thought-will, symbolized by the serpent and united toward a clarified end.

In an empowering innovation, Lévi explained how this élan vital, this vital force, for which the era had been searching, dwells within the individual where it is summoned by desire, symbol, ceremony, image, and allegory. Power is retained by reserve and focus; it is diluted by excess and dispersal, which is why the great magickian counseled abiding insight, wish, and occult operation in silence.

The Basics

Since my interest is reducing all steps in this book to practical essentials, I approach methodology with the clearest, simplest, and most effective ritual I know to employ this universal force. Reflecting the opening of this chapter, it is sex transmutation as described with remarkable insight in *Think and Grow Rich* and other references in Hill's talks.

Hill's concept of sex transmutation shares tantalizing commonalities with the works I have just cited along with classical Tantra, Taoism, and Kabbalah. Years ago, I knew an orthodox rabbi who struggled with being gay. He felt impossibly divided between the Jewish traditionalism to which he had dedicated himself and living out his sexuality with honesty. My friend privately approached an ultra-conservative rabbi in Israel and asked what do to. "My child," the elder said, "you have been given the sexuality of both a man and a woman. Use it carefully." Within this, I heard a subtle call to power.

Hill's historical inspiration may appear in a passage from Plato's *Symposium*, as translated by Victoriana's great man of letters, Benjamin Jowett (1817–1893). Socrates recounts the mysterious prophetess Diotima describing the powers of Eros, deity of passion and eroticism:

> He [Eros] is a great spirit (daimon), and like all spirits he is intermediate between... gods and men, conveying and taking across to the gods the prayers and sacrifices of men, and to men the commands and replies of the gods; he is the mediator who spans the chasm... For God mingles not with man; but through Love [Eros] all the intercourse and converse of God with man, whether awake or asleep, is carried on.

Hill's method of sex transmutation is simplicity itself. Experience has taught me that it works. As Hill saw it, the force of life seeking expression is experienced as the sexual urge. The same outlook appeared in the correspondence of Christian mystic and psychic Edgar Cayce (1877–1945) who in December 1935 wrote to a cousin who also told him of being gay: "That your experience has brought you manifestations that have at times, or often, expressed themselves in sex is not to be wondered at, when we realize that that is the expression of creative life on earth." As a side note, those who perceive occultism as a reactive social force in the twentieth century grossly oversimplify a social-spiritual revivalist movement that often proved personally liberating in the experience of the individual and gave expression to emancipatory social themes. There is no one-note understanding of occultism's social impact.

Returning to sexuality, the sexual urge is the sensate experience driving our species toward procreation and self-expression. As such, it is proves extremely, arguably overwhelmingly, powerful. Sexuality brings great joy and suffering, great harmony and conflict. It is above all the essential creative urge. It is the life force pursuing expansion. This holds true not only on a biological level but on all levels.

Humans are generative by nature. We build things, foster households, maintain commerce, solve problems, and create new ones. We devise technologies and seek, with greater and lesser success, to manage crises that accompany them. We raze old and erect new. All of these urges, Hill and others observed, are the force of life seeking expression. That force, experienced on the most primal level, is sexuality. Whenever you develop something, whether financial, artistic, architectural, craft-based, or product-based, this same life force is replicating itself through you.

Hill taught that you can harness and direct this energy wherever you wish—*and in a manner that contributes greater power, enthusiasm, perseverance, insight, intuition, logic, and acumen to any productive effort, including experiencing insights attributable to a sixth-sense mode of cognition.*

It works like this: Whenever you experience the sexual urge, at times of your private choosing, you mentally redirect your desire towards an expression other than the physical. You do this through the intellectual act of consciously rerouting your sexual impulse from physical to creative expression. This takes the shape of whatever your wish or effort is at the given moment. This act of transmutation is sexual alchemy.

Hill is not counseling sublimation or repression of the sexual urge. When I described sex transmutation to comedian and podcaster Duncan Trussell, he exclaimed, "Don't tell me I can't jerk off!" No worries. We can all jerk off. Hill noted there exists no greater tonic than sexuality for mood, stress relief, and physical relaxation. This reflected a liberated attitude in 1937. Rather, there exist channels through which sexual energy is expressed beyond physicality.

Sex Energy

Hill posits that greatly effective people in any area of life—the entrepreneur, the person who excels at a certain art, craft or science, the writer, the actor, the teacher, people who perform at a uniquely high level in their field, and those who evince magnetism and charisma—all of them, often unconsciously, are using sexual energy.

They are channeling the sexual urge, at critical moments, into their outer efforts. This imbues work and persona with greater vigor, substance, and appeal. This is true of all great salespeople:

you know you are being sold something; but you like (or feel subtly or overtly attracted) to him or her—and take the bait. That is sex transmutation, though often without conscious knowledge of the person wielding it.

Hill takes matters further and maintains that people widely considered geniuses, icons, and impresarios are able to rise to that level because sexual energy is at the back of their efforts; although, again, they may be unaware of the power under their command.

For the plural geniuses, Hill used the arcane *genii*. Genii dates to Roman-Latin usage. It means not only intellectual prowess but also suggests the ancient Roman meaning that genius is a gift bestowed by spirits, genii, or daemons. (In the Middle Ages, the Latin daemon referred to worker-bee spirits, neither intrinsically good nor bad.) The same term appears as jinn or genie in Arab folklore and culture, again as a spirit capable of bestowing supernatural power on the individual. This suggests the connection Hill rightly detected in ancient literature between higher forces of life or Eros and the individual's capacity for accomplishment.

Toward the end of his life, pioneering psychical researcher Frederic Myers (1843–1901) similarly pondered the nature and origin of genius. The British scientist came to believe that genius, or remarkable inspiration and application, possessed origin beyond localized intellect. Myers called it the supraliminal mind. In his posthumous 1903 treatise *Human Personality and Its Survival of Bodily Death*, the scientist wrote:

> Genius—if that vaguely used word is to receive anything like a psychological definition—should rather

be regarded as a power of utilising a wider range than other men can utilise of faculties in some degree innate in all;—a power of appropriating the results of subliminal mentation to subserve the supraliminal stream of thought;—so that an "inspiration of Genius" will be in truth a subliminal uprush, an emergence into the current of ideas which the man is consciously manipulating of other ideas which he has not consciously originated, but which have shaped themselves beyond his will, in profounder regions of his being. I shall urge that there is here no real departure from normality; no abnormality, at least in the sense of degeneration; but rather a fulfilment of the true norm of man, with suggestions, it may be, of something supernormal;—of something which transcends existing normality as an advanced stage of evolutionary progress transcends an earlier stage.

In short, Myers saw genius as interplay of subliminal / subconscious mind—a concept he helped establish—and a supraliminal mind, or what Hill termed Infinite Intelligence, comparable to *Nous* in Hermeticism. In Myers' view, this interplay produces genius, a perspective that jibes with Hill's.

Beat author William S. Burroughs (1914–1997), who knew Hill's work, advocated research into practical applications of the sex-energy concept of orgone, pioneered in the 1930s by Austrian-American psychoanalyst Wilhelm Reich (1897–1957). Although it can be reasonably asked whether Hill was aware of Reich's ideas, especially given the corresponding timeline, I have found no such evidence. Indeed, I have pored over Hill's life and work and discerned no definitive giveaway of his sources.

The Method Recapped

To leave no question regarding the steps of sex transmutation, I am recapping it. You can use this technique almost immediately.

When you experience sexual desire, at times and places of your own choosing, you mentally redirect the urge toward accomplishment of a valued task. Make the mental effort to channel sexual desire along different lines. Simply shift your thoughts away from physical sexual gratification toward another goal, e.g., completion of a piece of writing; pursuit of a client; design of a digital product; creation of your art; achievement of a physical or athletic goal—whatever it is, you act with the redirected sexual urge focused on your task or aim.

The point is not creating another orthodoxy or "rule" around sex. Sometimes physical expression must be honored. Sexual activity, for pleasure or procreation, is critical for mental, emotional, and physical wellness, as well as for propagation. But in private moments that you alone choose, you can mentally redirect your sexual desire toward a specific task or activity. I have, for example, used sex transmutation in writing this very chapter.

Once you have successfully attempted this you may discover new and varying ways of employing sex transmutation. For example, you can use sex transmutation to cultivate a specific mood or personality trait, such as confidence, courage, or enthusiasm.

You may attempt this in the near-term for help with a job interview or to face down a bully; or you may want to use this practice in the long term to remake an aspect of your personality, appearance, or to help someone in crisis. Set no fixed limits on what you may find.

As British occultist and artist Aleister Crowley recorded in 1904 in *The Book of the Law*: "Success is thy proof."

CHAPTER FOUR

The Power of a Single Wish

I want to be very careful with how I word this chapter. My contention is that a clarified wish can deliver you to unimagined shores. But I mean a certain kind of wish possessed of remarkable self-honesty.

It is the only kind of wish deserving the name.

I believe we are alienated from our truest wishes. By this I mean, we internalize custom and peer pressure to the degree of conditioning even our most intimate communications within. As a result, we obfuscate what we really want to express, attain, or perform in life. We substitute recitation for sincerity, embarrassment for earnestness.

Let's say you encounter the proverbial genie in a lamp. He offers you one—and only one—wish. Your wish will come true, but only if you are entirely sincere and self-honest. Otherwise, you will lose everything. What is it?

This chapter ventures a deadly serious approach to this question. Any reader seeking spiritual mind-candy, "life hacks" (banish that term from our vernacular), or are *you-are-good-enough* bromides, should stop reading.

In matters of personal philosophy, I believe that knowing *why* something works is tantamount *to it working*. Hence, this chapter considers the power of a wish intently and in detail. If that sounds appealing, and only if, you are in the right company.

What Do You Want?

Twentieth-century spiritual philosopher G.I. Gurdjieff had many remarkable and enterprising students. Among the most impressive was English writer and editor A.R. Orage (1873–1934), a working-class man of letters whose thought touched the modern West both spiritually and socially. Historian J. Walter Driscoll wrote of Orage in the spring 1998 *Gurdjieff International Review*:

> Equipped with the barest formal education, a formidable natural intelligence and an unquenchable yearning to understand, Alfred Richard Orage emerged from British 19th century working class poverty to survey the significant literary, psychological, political and spiritual trends of the early 20th century. His literary skills and wide range of interests led him to edit the enormously influential journal the *New Age* from 1907 until 1922 when he moved from London to Fontainebleau to attend Gurdjieff's Institute for the Harmonious Development of Man.

Orage produced an under-recognized classic of self-development, published in 1930 as *The Active Mind: Adventures in Awareness* and reissued in 1965 as *Psychological Exercises and Essays*. In it, the seeking author noted our daily inattention to our "native tastes":

You wake in the morning and propose to get up. Ask yourself whether you really wish to get up. And be candid about it. You take a bath—is it really because you like it or would dodge it if you could? You eat your breakfast—is it exactly the breakfast you like—in kind and quantity? Is it just your breakfast you eat, or simply breakfast as defined by society? Do you, in fact, wish to eat at all? You go to your office, or being a woman, you set about domestic and social duties of the day—are they your native tastes? Would you of your own free choice be where you are and do what you do? Assuming that, for the present, you accept the general situation, are you in detail doing what you like? Do you speak as it pleases you to this, that or the other persons? Do you really like or only pretend to like them? (Remember that it is not a question yet of acting on your likes and dislikes but only of discovering what they are really). You pass the day, every phase offering a new opportunity for self-questioning—do I really like this or not? The evening arrives with leisure—what would you really like to do? What truly amuses you, theatre or movies, conversation, reading, music, games, and exactly which? It cannot be repeated too often that the doing of what you like comes later. In fact, it can be left to take care of itself. The important thing is to know what you like.

The method here suggested may seem trivial to those accustomed to the extravagances of the "literature of revolt" but we undertake to say that a week of it would convince everybody of its magical efficiency.

Pay close attention to Orage's observation that you need not lapse into distraction over the question of *acting* on your wishes, whether practical or impractical, possible or impossible. The question of "how" is a diversion that stymies awareness and acknowledgment. *How* often proves an excuse for inertia in matters of attention and desire, a point to which we return.

The Power of a Wish

My journey into the question and meaning of a wish began as do many experiments in ethical and spiritual philosophy: with a memory.

Many years ago, during my publishing career I was an acquisitions editor at a now-dead political imprint called The Free Press (not to be confused with the more recent news outlet). The imprint, newly bought by Simon & Schuster, was floundering. The man who made it great had left (and suddenly died) rather than work for the new owners. Meetings droned on about the need for fresh directions. I am often leery of media outlets announcing novel initiatives. I believe that most problems are solved by mastering the basics, which few people take the time to do.

At a weekly editorial-board meeting, a colleague mentioned that an accomplished literary journalist—I do not recall who—wanted to write a nonfiction book on the power of a wish. The latest publisher, a nattily dressed and easily triggered man who harbored suspicion toward me and other staffers ("*Conservative books don't sell, Mitch!*" he once yelled), perked up and said that he thought it sounded like a good idea. I heartily agreed.

The book, to my knowledge, never got written. But its theme haunted me. The unrecalled journalist was, to my understanding, approaching this study of wishes from a non-spiritual perspective. But what, after all, is spiritual or non-spiritual? I believe that our lives traverse both mundane and extra-physical spheres, evidence of which appears, for example, in widely replicated lab studies of ESP, precognition, and telepathy.

The verity of extra-physicality informs my exploration. There exists a discernable bridge between psi phenomena and the passion of desire. As historian of religions Jeffrey J. Kripal—my own Professor X—wrote me in early 2022, "The notion that 'passion is critical' is embedded in the coinage of the term 'telepathy' or 'pathos at a distance' and not 'indifferent neutrality at a distance.' [F.W.H.] Myers, in fact, linked telepathy to eros." As Jeff alludes—and repeated lab experiments and field studies support—passion is the lever for extra-physical communication when it fitfully, although sometimes with jarring vividness, occurs; knowing your passions abets a measure of awareness around this process.

In Jeff's 2010 *Authors of the Impossible*, he quotes nineteenth-century scientist and parapsychology pioneer Myers (1843–1901) from his posthumous 1903 classic *Human Personality and Its Survival of Bodily Death*: "Love is a kind of exalted, but unspecialized telepathy," adding his own observation that "the French word for 'magnet' is, quite literally, 'lover' (*amant*)." If it is possible to psychically reach the dead, this facet of nonlocal existence, Jeff surmises, is "how Love finally conquered Death."

Napoleon Hill, sensing the connection between telepathy and pathos, wrote presciently in *Think and Grow Rich*, with emphasis his: "*Mental telepathy is a reality.* Thoughts pass from one mind to another, voluntarily, whether or not this fact is recognized by either the person releasing the thoughts, or the persons who pick up those thoughts."

The Long Road

It may not surprise you that The Free Press soon fired me. I decamped, with some personal strain, to an imprint specializing in the kinds of New Age and metaphysical literature better suited to my tastes and instincts. The move was a significant step-down in prestige as *The New Yorker* was not reviewing many books on the enneagram—but for reasons of pragmatism and a gradual sense of mission, I soon felt at home.

At what was then called TarcherPenguin, I rose to the position of corporate vice president and division editor in chief. Early in my efforts, I issued the work of a widely read psychic about whose character I felt uncertain but whose capacity for foresight I considered actual and still do. One night, we were having a conversation and she said, "Do you know what you want? You want power. But you have an overdeveloped superego." I recoiled from her insight and spent years rejecting it.

Let me say a further word about psychical abilities. Groundbreaking graphic artist and occultist Austin Osman Spare (1886–1956) wrote in his 1954 *Formulae of Zos Vel Thanatos*: "Many experiences I cannot reproduce and in some cases even re-vision." This may offer a yellow light to those who visit by-the-hour psychics. As alluded, I believe in the actuality of psychical insight. But such insight cannot, in my estimation, be turned on and off like a water tap. This is why J.B. Rhine, the preeminent dean of psychical research and one of my intellectual heroes, stopped working with professional psychics in the mid-1960s.

I knew another channel or psychic in my publishing days who gave me vital and, I believe, veritable advice that rescued me from a work crisis causing health-threatening anxiety. In short, he told me—rightly—to immediately sever all ties with a thuggish author: the kind who wears a lobbyist's suit, wants to save the world, and produces no end of misery for all around him. When my friend delivered this reading, his face astonishingly assumed the features of the subject. Trusting my psychic source, I returned to him about year later with a question of deep intimacy. He encouraged me to confess my feelings to another, which I foolishly and selfishly did: the fallout almost ended my life, liberty, and happiness. This, I believe, is why a highly accomplished spiritual publisher once cautioned: "You should doubt 50 percent of what a psychic tells you."

Recent to this writing, I commented on X:

> Parapsychology as a field is never going to be without controversy in my lifetime. It tests for the existence of a bridge of mechanics and phenomena between physics and cognition. The primary manner in which to pursue this question is testing for experimental evidence. The best of this replicable evidence—e.g., Rhine, Honorton, Stevenson, Radin, Bem, et al.—is methodologically and mathematically world-class science...

In something of non sequitur, a "metaphysical consultant" responded:

> Observer ("Participator") Effect is why "legit psychics" don't bother w/skeptical White Coats & their tests/experiments. Consciousness can easily change outcomes outside of time/space, so even if a psychic demonstrated something, results could be shifted/negated. Waste of time.

The commenter raises a valid point—to a degree. Her principle also functions as a covers-all-bases insurance policy against getting it wrong. Suggesting that extremes form a circle, this statement coalesces with one from twentieth-century psi-buster and pseudo-skeptic James Randi (1928–2020): "I always have an 'out'—I'm right!"* (I should note that many psychics participated gainfully in Project Stargate, considered in Appendix A.)

For all that, I take seriously the psychical prospect. Following the perspective of years, I had to acknowledge the truth behind my earlier psychical accessor's insight, whatever its source, about my wish for power. I distinguish power from force. I saw my colleague as a forceful and aggressive person—I did not want power in that sense. I wanted the power of a thought leader. And, with it, recognition and remuneration. There is no time, if one values a seat on the lifeboat, for perfumed or precious attitudes. When facing existential questions, I neither accept nor proffer catechistic responses, often based on translations of translations of wisdom literature. I want truth as felt in body and psyche. I consider the latter a compact of thought and emotion. Truth is vulnerable and slightly embarrassing. It requires self-verification, not in principle but actually.

Can't Buy You Love?

Sufi teacher Hazrat Inayat Khan (1882–1927), a great twentieth-century figure who helped bring Sufism to the West, was asked by an English-speaking student whether it is necessary to give up riches in order to attain realization. Hazrat replied, "You do not have riches—how can you give up what is not yours?"

---

* See "The Man Who Destroyed Skepticism" in my *Uncertain Places: Essays on Occult and Outsider Experiences* (Inner Traditions, 2022).

I must digress to offer inadequate tribute to the Khan family. In addition to Sufi teacher Pir Vilayat (1916–2004), who I was privileged to know, Hazrat was father to Noor Inayat Khan (1914–1944). While the Khans were dedicated to nonviolence—although Muslim they followed Gandhi's initiative—Noor volunteered for service in the French Resistance during World War II. She was captured and executed at Dachau. Enough cannot be said about the bravery and decency of this woman. She is the subject of a justly detailed article at Wikipedia. Her brother Pir Vilayat, who had also taken a vow of nonviolence, enlisted as a sailor on a mine-sweeper in the Royal Navy. Pir recalled that his practice of meditation made him an especially good watchman.

To return to Hazrat's injunction, anyone who contends, absent investigation, that worldly success cannot make you happy either has never experienced that success or has spent his or her life chasing it, finding it, and would never give it up—despite holding forth on its limits.

Some spiritual traditions and their modern exponents teach that we lack self-perspective and are too divided within to speak of possessing or understanding authentic wishes, especially of a worldly nature. Experience has taught me to dissent from that judgment. I believe that at certain sensitive moments, we, as individuals, possess higher perspective—not ultimate but higher. We are not the victims of a cosmic joke that deters us from knowing ourselves and what we truly want. Released from peer pressure and conditioning, we are more mature and self-availing than we realize.

One July 4th weekend, I made the slightly giddy offer of free Tarot readings to my social-media followers. The response was overwhelming. I did hundreds of three-card readings in about seventy-two hours. I noticed that nearly every question involved career, romance, health, and—a distant fourth—inner development. Those are facts of our lives not to be explained away or apologized for. I make no division in my search between higher and lower, white magick and black magick, inner and outer—I see no means of determining lines of demarcation among each nor evaluating the difference in the life of another since motive often proves subtler than choice.

Pushback against aspirational wishes in both spiritual and literary culture can produce ironic and nearly humorous results. In 2019, *The New York Times* op-ed page published an essay by a Princeton University writing instructor arguing against the "desire for greatness" and extolling the ethic of being "good enough." This is a popular theme among social critics, including philosopher Christopher Lasch (1932–1994) and bestselling columnist David Brooks. How did the "good enough" essay land on that coveted page? Its author won first-place in an essay-writing contest sponsored by the Brooklyn Public Library. This was noted without irony.

My point is: deal with actualities. Forget about "what seems," "what ifs" or what some historic personage, tradition, or custom says. This is your life. The answer of who you are and what you want may vastly differ from what internalized culture, ritualized habit, or peer pressure induces you to repeat.

I stress the ethic of self-honesty. In my view, every mature, seeking person is capable of sincerely answering: *what do you want?* I believe that many spiritual and therapeutic traditions and gatekeepers *deprive the individual* of that question—and make it seem as though he or she is unable to identify a core self because we are in pieces within. And this holds truth. Emotions, intellect, physicality, and sexuality are all running riot on their own. But the notion that the individual is unable to know what he or she wants is, I think, fallacy. I believe that any emotionally sensitive twelve-year-old could tell you what he or she wants without didactic qualification. I do not believe such realization should be taken from that person.

You might be surprised by what you want. In the confounding (and, I think, brilliant) 2024 Nicole Kidman thriller *Baby Girl*, the protagonist, a high-powered CEO, discovers, after a life pursuing corporate leadership, that she wants to be told what to do. That certainly is not all that she wants but it reflects—especially sexually—an unacknowledged facet of self.

Kidman's character, Romy, lets slip early in the movie that she was named by a guru and grew up in cults in a presumptive atmosphere of control. That early childhood experience, I reckon, colored her sense of intimacy and sexual desire, as do all early experiences, especially at periods of sexual awakening. For Romy, subjugation fused with sexuality. Trying to alter arousal is, I think, as futile as trying to change eye color. Magickian Anton LaVey (1930–1997) called our early arousal points Erotic Crystallization Inertia or ECI—understanding it is of great help in magick, affirmation, and visualization. Points of arousal are highly individualized, sometimes curious and sometimes confounding, and should never be fought but accommodated within contours of self-respect and consent.

To use a different example, maybe you have dedicated your life to pursuing pure learning, which is a noble aim—yet what you really want is money. Money does a lot of good things. I think gross consumption usually points to an unhappiness or gap in the individual. So maybe the person involved in gross consumption does not really want money. These are maybes. But we rarely grant ourselves the opportunity to really ask.

The *Feeling* of a Wish

As is clear by now, if I have one inviolate rule in the search, it is a *clarified wish*. I urge unprejudiced and even uncomfortable acknowledgment of your innermost aspirations. I suggest revisiting your earliest memories, around ages three or four, to uncover authentic desires that predate full-on social conditioning. This period is critical, marking the genesis of long-term memories and galvanized dreams and wishes. Turn back these layers and ask, with unadulterated honesty, what you wanted then—and want now—free from shackles of embarrassment or moral judgment, which generally amount to little more than internalized peer pressure or fear. The congruity may surprise you.

Again, this effort of introspection must remain untainted by social labels or expectations. Looking back on my search, I find that deeply felt wishes I harbored as a child have appeared, albeit over a considerable span of time, such as speaking and communicating in public—including the words you are now reading.

What I suggest aligns with Goethe's insight, indirectly considered in his matchless iteration of *Faust*, that the wishes of youth, for good or ill, emerge unexpectedly as we age. Recognizing and honoring these wishes, shielded from peer influence, is paramount. The path to self-discovery and activation of personal power often commences with this simple yet profound act: internally (and accurately) acknowledging your radically honest, unabashed wish.

Clarity of intent, in my experience, concentrates power and catalyzes change, whether immediately or over time. This is a natural law inasmuch as particles or droplets densely concentrated form a near-irresistible force.

THE POWER OF A SINGLE WISH

* * *

Let me share a private episode that galvanized so much in my current life. On a winter afternoon about eighteen years ago, I climbed to the top of a stone tower on the banks of the Charles River in Weston, Massachusetts. The Victorian-era oddity (or folly as the style is sometimes known) was built in 1889 to commemorate a Viking settlement that some believe Norse explorer Leif Erikson founded on the banks of the Charles around 1,000 A.D. (In terms of historical accuracy, I can note only that a viable waterway, the Charles and St. Lawrence Rivers, connects the area to Leif's probable touchdown in Newfoundland, Canada.)

Named Norumbega Tower, after the reputed settlement, the thirty-eight-foot column had iron bars on its windows and doors to keep out snoopers, ghost hunters, and pentagram-spraying heavy-metal kids (may השטן love them). All I knew was that I wanted to go inside. I slithered my six-foot-two-inch frame through a loose grill, discovered some graffiti left by said metalheads and climbed a dank spiral stairway to the top.

At that time in life, I had one great desire burning in my veins: to become a writer. I had already been active in that direction, but I was not young—I was past forty. I swore from the top of that tower that I would establish myself as a known author. I asked all forces available to me on that frigid day, seen and unseen, physical and extraphysical, to come to my aid.

Something swelled within me at that moment: I felt in sync physically, intellectually, and emotionally, and at one with my surroundings; my wish resounded clear, strong, and assured, as though lifted by an unseen current. It was a totalizing experience, which went beyond the common. In the years immediately ahead,

I did become known as a writer—I was published by Random House and other presses, won a PEN literary award, and received bylines in publications such as *The New York Times, The Wall Street Journal, The Washington Post,* and *Politico*—outlets rarely drawn, and often culturally averse, to my occult themes.

My act that winter day was entirely spontaneous, neither planned nor prepared for. Nor was I reciting ceremonies, spells, or rituals from another's playbook.

Some years later, I had a related experience. I was suffering a sense of failure in my efforts to break into television and movies. I yearned to host or otherwise present occult or paranormal themes on screen with integrity and intellect. "What you want," a trusted colleague cautioned, "requires a revolution in our culture." Well, that is what I wanted. In July 2017, I wrote these words in the margin of my dogeared paperback of *Think and Grow Rich* (covered in clear packing tape for durability): "My TV plans have not been sound—I am at cross purposes. I need a new vision of what will work, and what is right / compatible with my ideals."

Just around that time, I visited the Museum of the Moving Image in Astoria, Queens, in New York. As part of the exhibit that summer day, movie-set trailers were parked out front and visitors were allowed to enter makeup and holding rooms typically used by on-set actors. Inside the museum (in addition to a life-size, head-rotating doll from *The Exorcist*) appears a delightful walk-in exhibit that expressionistically replicates the interior of vintage movie palaces. I found myself alone in that space. It was a propitious moment in which I felt emotion welling up in me. I again prayed to all forces within and without to bring me the screen success for which I yearned. I repeated something similar when I entered—and stole moments of privacy in—the location trailers.

The road that followed was hard, twisting, and, at times, sufficiently difficult so that days occurred where I vowed to give it up. In a park on New York's Lower East Side, after suffering betrayal on a screen project from someone I had considered a close friend, I wrote in my notebook on April 21, 2021: "My DCA [Definite Chief Aim] has failed. It is eating me alive. I need a turn of corner... I need a new DCA. TV is not viable. Kybalion movie = headed south."

But an authentic wish is a strange thing: you cannot give it up. It owns you. You are indebted to it. Hours or at most a day later, the wish came roaring back, as it had other times. On April 23, 2021, I wrote: "I cannot move away from my DCA."

As I write this, I have a development deal with the A&E Channel. I host a Discovery / HBO Max show, *Alien Encounters*, which spent three weeks in Max's top-ten TV shows. I play myself as a historical commentator in the latest installment of AMC-Shudder's found-footage horror franchise V/H/S/BEYOND, which was nominated for a 2025 Critics Choice Award for Best Movie Made for Television (laurels to segment director Jay Cheel). I play a newscaster in the Sundance-premiering 2023 Paramount thriller *My Animal* directed by Jacqueline Castel. I am featured in the 2024 docuseries *Beyond: UFOs and the Unknown* on MGM+, executive produced by J.J. Abrams. My 2022 feature documentary *The Kybalion*, brilliantly directed by Emmy-nominee Ronni Thomas and shot on location in Egypt, premiered as the number-three documentary on iTunes. I have ethical management at SpectreVision, a media company cofounded by actor Elijah Wood. Jim Perry, Daniel Noah and other principals there collaborated with me on a dream-come-true podcast, *Extraordinary Evidence: ESP Is Real*. I appear regularly on *The UnBelievable with Dan Aykroyd* on the History Channel. In a November 15, 2024, interview with

Decider, Dan said: "I love Mitch Horowitz. He's great... I kind of relate to him in a way. I just like his look, you know?" While moving by itself, Dan's comment arrived several months after producers at a production company told my manager they were unhappy with my leather-jacketed look. They pressed him to lie and say it was his idea that my leather go. He refused. Thank you, Antonio D'Intino. During this writing, I became an on-camera expert for the History Channel show *The Proof Is Out There*. I also shot a substantial interview for another network's forthcoming occult-themed, true-crime series. Days prior to completing this chapter, I shot a pilot for History—and so on.

The effort never stops and arrival is always tantalizingly a step away—but progress? In early 2024, when I stepped into the talent trailer on the Roswell, New Mexico, set of *Alien Encounters*, the sense of symmetry was uncanny and emotional. My eyes teared.

In addition to enormous and longstanding effort—my first major TV appearance dates to the *Montel Williams Show* in 2007 (we discussed the world ending in 2012, which it apparently did not)—I attribute this progress, as with my writing, to the power of a passionately felt, clarified wish followed through with tremendous sweat equity. In each case, my wish provided momentum, focus, and, I believe, some measure of the selective and telepathic agencies I reference earlier. Some will cry "confirmation bias" (a finger always pointed outward). My warranty stems from as much enduring effort and perspective as a seeking person can muster.

I believe that a single wish and laser-focus works best. This is what Napoleon Hill called a Definite Chief Aim, as referenced earlier. But I also recognize that one wish realized (if not wholly completed) can be followed by another, *especially in relation to the first*. That, at least, is my personal approach. Should life throw at you something dramatically unexpected and urgent, a wish may of necessity change or grow. The point is not creating new orthodoxies (on which I gag) but responding to authentic passions.

Some argue that life's myriad demands render it impossible to select a single wish. As noted, concentration produces impact. Bear in mind: one wish can cover a lot of bases in life. Your wish is not tantamount to turning your back on other needs and relationships. Irrigation channels branch off from your wish.

But *How?*

Before offering an exercise to clarify your wish, I must revisit the question of "how." I contend that an authentic wish—barring extreme countervailing measures or emergencies—is innately practicable. A wish is neither pipe dream nor fantasy. We often cry *"how?"* not because we have tried and failed but because we intend never to try.

Let the person who has tried and failed ten times approach me or another with the question of "how?" Anything less is inertia, which is the modus operandi for which most people settle, at least those who can retreat behind conditions of relative ease. This retreat produces the ennui that drives many of us into repeat-loops of talk therapy, bellyaching to a shrink about this and that quotidian woe without once confronting the crisis back of it all: paucity of self-expression. I hope I do not seem coarse. But barring extreme tragedy or macro-crises beyond individual influence, I see this pattern among most people in settings of reasonable comfort.

Once upon a time, I wrote on Twitter, "Excellence is your only defense." A reader replied, "The question then is, how does one achieve excellence?" For that, I lean on a intellect far greater than mine.

In 1964, the unclassifiable spiritual teacher Jiddu Krishnamurti (1895–1986) conducted a series of dialogues with young students in India. It appears in his book *Think on These Things*. The teacher spoke of the dulling effect of conformity and the need to live by your inner compass. A boy asked him: "How can we put into practice what you are telling us?"

Krishnamurti replied that if you want something badly enough, you know exactly what to do. "When you meet a cobra on the road," the teacher said, "you don't ask 'What am I do to?' You understand very well the danger of a cobra and you stay away from it." Krishnamurti noted:

> You hear something which you think is right and you want to carry it out in your everyday life; so there is a gap between what you think and what you do, is there not? You think one thing, and you are doing something else. But you want to put into practice what you think, so there is this gap between action and thought; and then you ask how to bridge the gap, how to link your thinking to your action.
>
> Now, when you want to do something very much, you do it, don't you? When you want to go and play cricket, or do some other thing in which you are really interested, you find ways and means of doing it; you never ask how to put it into practice. You do it because you are eager, because your whole being, your mind and heart are in it.

Regardless, people make excuses why they cannot act on the one thing for which they long. They say they cannot possibly make a living at it or they do not know where to begin. Money is vital.

But money is often an alibi for inertia. You can always *begin* something. And it is critical that you not condition that beginning on quitting your day job, which may prove a lifelong fact of existence, a question I touch on in chapter eleven, "It Is Not Too Late."

In terms of life-work balance—a trope for the ennui generation—I knew that I would successfully complete my first book *Occult America* (2009), which I wrote while co-raising two young sons and holding down a corporate publishing job, when I realized that *I wanted to write more than I wanted to sleep*. That is unsustainable long-term. But for a fixed time, it proved workable. I wrote till my body crossed the point of physical fatigue, which arrives much later than we coddle ourselves to believe. When the body is truly tired, stop. Before then, all depends on what you really want; on whether your wish is real. We consider the nature of persistence in chapter six.

Let me return to Krishnamurti. Another Indian youth told the teacher that he feared being kicked out of his home if he violated his father's demands and pursued a career as an engineer. *Act*, Krishnamurti told the student, and life will rise to your demands:

> If you persist in wanting to be an engineer even though your father turns you out of the house, do you mean to say that you won't find ways and means to study engineering? You will beg, go to friends. Sir, life is very strange. The moment you are very clear about what you want to do, things happen. Life comes to your aid—a friend, a relation, a teacher, a grandmother, somebody helps you. But if you are afraid to try because your father may turn you out, then you are lost. Life never comes to the aid of those who merely yield to some

demand out of fear. But if you say, "This is what I really want to do and I am going to pursue it," then you will find that something miraculous takes place.

Philosopher Jacob Needleman (1934–2022) once asked me: "What do you do when someone offers you a gift?" After I stared at him blankly, he replied: "You accept it!" Krishnamurti's words are a gift.

Wishcraft

Based on what I have described, attempt this technique:

1. As you complete this chapter, or another time when you have privacy, ask—without embarrassment or self-censorship—what you truly want. It can be intimate, material, situational—anything. Your emotions must be in earnest. Damn all internalized peer pressure, "spiritual" ideals, or qualifications (and do not say "service" unless you are Albert Schweitzer). Be honest.

2. When identifying your wish, do not confuse means with ends. You do not necessarily need to focus on one singular path or solution. Things reach us by many roads. Do not hem yourself in.

3. Hold that wish. Speak it aloud. If you are alone, in nature, or on a platform as a train arrives, shout it.

4. Write it down. Clearly and plainly. Take the slip of paper or card on which you have written your wish and place it in your pocket. If possible, wrap it in clear packing tape (of which I am a fan) to protect it. Carry it like a talisman. The very act clarifies. And something more: writing your wish on paper provides a *particulate yet tangible nascency of realized desires.* Something is present that was not there before.

5. Run your wish through your mind as often as possible. Dote on it.
6. Pray for your wish to whatever Greater Force you seek a relationship with. (I explore this in *Practical Magick*.)
7. Recite your wish as you drift to sleep, i.e., in the highly suggestible, mentally subtle state of hypnagogia, explored in chapter two, and do so again as you awaken. Do not underestimate this.

Record what occurs. Try.

Abide Silence

In 2004, Bob Dylan made a valuable observation during a *60 Minutes* interview about his autobiography *Chronicles: Volume One*:

> ED BRADLEY: You use the word destiny over and over throughout the book. What does that mean to you?
>
> DYLAN: It's a feeling you have that you know something about yourself nobody else does. The picture you have in your mind of what you're about will come true. It's kinda the thing you kinda have to keep to your own self—because it's a fragile feeling and you put it out there, somebody will kill it. So, it's best to keep that all inside.

That is as good an explanation as I know for the importance of maintaining silence around your wishes and hallowed self-conceptions. In his 1856 *Doctrine and Ritual of High Magic*, occult revivalist Eliphas Lévi (1810–1875) explained how the elixer for which his mid-nineteenth-century generation had been searching dwells within the individual where it is aroused by desire, symbol, ceremony, image, and allegory. This power is retained by reserve and focus; it is diluted by excess and dispersal. Lévi provided a credo for the dawning magickal culture:

> One must KNOW in order to DARE.
> One must DARE in order to WILL.
> One must WILL to have the Empire.
> And to reign, one must BE SILENT.

Silence—it is the easiest treasure to hold and to squander. When harboring a key idea of self or plans, we often commit the knee-jerk error of seeking emotional validation, as I once did.

At one point in my publishing career, I dreamed of starting an independent press dedicated to classic, below-the-radar, and often public-domain reissues. I rigorously researched the market, copyright issues, and prevailing and unfolding technology. I never started the press but based on its premises devised a boundingly successful rediscovery program at Penguin Random House. One of my titles, a 2008 reissue of Napoleon Hill's *The Law of Success*, had a 77% gross-operating profit. This was not an errant occurrence. I used to say over and over: "When you sell one copy of a public-domain book you sell the budgetary equivalent of two because you keep all the money." The program rescued my imprint during the 2008 Great Recession, which shuttered the national book chain Borders. My proudest accomplishment is that no one at my shop lost their jobs during that harrowing period.

Sharing my vision of an indie reissue press with a close friend, however, I found he ran it down and diminished it with snide remarks. He sometimes dropped such asides into otherwise relaxed conversations, blindsiding me. In retrospect, I realize I was foolish. You cannot disclose treasured plans to another, whether friend or family, but only to professional colleagues with real expertise (who you might have to pay for it). An exception are close colleagues united in Hill's conception of a "Master Mind" group, a harmonious, liked-minded fellowship of mutual support.

Human nature often seeks to destroy or devalue what it cannot personally attain. Hence, when you disclose your wishes to another there exists likelihood—barring special circumstances—that he or she will either subtly or ham-fistedly attempt to shatter it.

Do not let that happen. Silence is your sword and shield.

Letter to an Inmate

Some of my critics consider me too materialistic and conventionally aspirational. I have been called "outer looking." I sometimes maintain correspondence with incarcerates. Here is a letter pertinent to that issue:

January 10, 2025

Dear Mike,

Thank you for your letter of November 12 and your birthday wishes.

You cover a lot of interesting ground in your note. In hopes this reply proves useful, I will share an element of my recent search. As you noted, I am unsentimental about wishes: I believe they must be clear, blunt, and unflinchingly self-honest. I also believe in reciprocal ethics.

In my mid-thirties, I discovered the work of spiritual philosopher G.I. Gurdjieff to which I dedicated about eight years of group effort. I treasure the experience daily. The question of what one wants from the work was always a hot-button issue for me. I am clear about what I want; one can read it in *Daydream Believer* or elsewhere. My search is pretty public for the sake of exchanging transparently with readers.

I have lately revisited a passage from *In Search of the Miraculous*, P.D. Ouspensky's invaluable record of his time with Gurdjieff. In it, the teacher asks a circle of students to state their personal aims and what they desire from the work. The answers are fairly ordinary: world peace, to know the future, immortality, to be a real Christian, and so forth. In short, Gurdjieff replies:

> *Of the desires expressed the one which is most right is the desire to be master of oneself, because without this nothing else is possible. And in comparison with this desire all other desires are simply childish dreams, desires of which a man could make no use even if they were granted to him.*

For many years, I resisted his formulation. It did not stir my passions. It seemed too far away. (The more involved one becomes with the work, the further and further it seems, almost to the point of impossibility. Only those who have been stripped of fantasies about self can understand that.)

I used to, and in some ways still do, pose an exercise to others and myself. Let's say you encounter the proverbial genie in a lamp. He offers you one—and just one—wish. Your wish will be granted, but only if you are entirely self-honest about what you want. If you are not, you will lose everything. What is it?

I despise treacly responses and set up this question to get down to the emotional skin-and-bone of things. I often say that life strikes a tough bargain with us: we are granted the one thing we want above all else, whether we admit it to ourselves. People object: I have so many needs and obligations; how can I boil it all down to one thing? I say that one well-selected aim can cover a lot of bases: so choose carefully.

Lately, I have been newly posing this genie question to myself. I find that I am starting to sound a little bit like my interlocutors. I have many bases to cover and I want to ensure that no one I love (of whom there are few) gets left behind. Hence, I am thinking anew about Gurdjieff's demand. Is being "master of oneself" possible? Probably not. But this aim fulfilled would allow someone to actually place hands on the levers granted us—and find his or her way in the world, something impossible for someone controlled and contorted entirely by external influences, i.e., all but a very few of us, if any.

I share this by way of exchange. I am happy to send you a copy of this book if you like.

Wishing you all good things,
Mitch

Perhaps this would prove an august note on which to end. But if I practice the same honesty with you that I urge you to practice with yourself, I must be plain. In the five months that have passed since I sent that letter, my wishes remain as passionate—and aspirational—as earlier.

As alluded, and without sentimentality, a wish choses us not us it. I nonetheless abide the passage above as food for your journey and mine.

I end, finally, on the words of nineteenth-century Swiss ethicist Henri-Frédéric Amiel (1821–1881), who in 1857 wrote in his journals: "Without passion man is a mere latent force and possibility, like the flint which awaits the shock of the iron before it can give forth its spark."*

Go tell yourself the truth of your most deeply felt passion. There will appear your wish. And with it, very likely, your life.

---

* Translated in 1885 by British novelist and social reformer Mary Augusta Ward (1851–1920).

CHAPTER FIVE

Escape Predatory Personalities

I want to open this chapter with a word of exceedingly—and deceptively—simple advice that Napoleon Hill delivered in a transcribed but undated and unpublished talk: "Avoid persons and circumstances which make you feel inferior."

This simple remark contains greater dimensions than may at first appear. As noted in chapter one, ESP researcher J.B. Rhine, and others following him, emphasized the need for a supportive environment if the nonlocal capacities of the mind or sixth sense are going to occur. This is a general truth of life: intuition, growth, and creativity flounder in environments of hostility.

In 1945, Hill sounded this principle in *The Master Key to Riches*:

> One must remove himself from the range of influence of every person and every circumstance which has even a slight tendency to cause him to feel inferior or incapable of attaining the object of his purpose. Positive egos do not grow in negative environments. On this point there can be no excuse for a compromise, and failure to observe it will prove fatal to the chance of success.

One of the toughest lessons I have had to learn in life, and that I am still learning as I write these words, is the vital importance of this step. It is complicated by the general prevalence of people who are *emotionally predatory*. Such people use emotional power plays—almost always with plausible deniability—to keep you unsteady, needful, or confused. Emotional power plays are vampiric. Such moves are the adjunct reality for which the mythical vampire is metaphor. They must be watched for and, when discovered, separated from.

What I am writing took on a greater sense of urgency to me recently. I realized that the predatory personality—and I write this based on no data beyond personal observation—probably composes something like fifty percent of the population.

Shocking as that hypothesis sounds (although less so when perusing social media), it is why our culture abounds with terms like narcissist, bully, crazy maker, abuser, borderline personality, and so on. These terms and others denote the emotional predator, whose aim, sometimes unconsciously—which is of no pragmatic importance in terms of conduct—is to use force over another or derive a sense of power from another's suffering.

Sometimes this thirst for force arises from a creative, physical, intimate, or financial deficit for which the aggressor compensates by destructive domination. The key thing is not to analyze this dynamic so much as to avoid it.

There exists a subset of this predatory personality, which might be identified under the rubric of *parasitical versus creative*. This variant appears in those who attach themselves to projects, institutions, or people to receive reflected glory. The thing sought may be reputation, image, opportunity, or money. There is nothing wrong with any of that provided another party *authentically contributes* to the quality of what is produced and thus benefits symbiotically. The danger with the parasitical personality is that months or even years can pass before its nature as a taker versus a contributor becomes clear.

Predatory personalities are often cognitively and emotionally sophisticated. They may sustain periods of friendship and even intimacy for months or years: for as long as the arrangement delivers what they need. Despite the simulation of bonding, however, this person does not experience empathy.

The predatory personality can read emotions—*but the only emotions that this persona experiences are his or her own.* Hence, such figures often prove insightful, shrewd, and possessed of well-constructed self-justification. They may even conceal their motives from themselves. In George MacDonald Fraser's ribald novel *Flashman* (1969), the antihero says: "I have observed, in the course of a dishonest life, that when a rogue is outlining a treacherous plan, he works harder to convince himself more than to move his hearers."

This dynamic also reveals why people sometimes form business partnerships only to discover years into their effort that their collaborator—someone who is perhaps a godparent to their kids, a personal confidant, or an advice-giver—has skimmed profits or committed fraud. This is sometimes revealed through a single event or gets detected across the arc of a pattern. When the reality comes to light, it creates so great a break with perception that the victim cannot immediately digest it. When digestion eventually occurs, and damage is assessed and mitigated, the betrayal itself may remain partly undigested, perhaps for a lifetime. This is understandable. The feeling that someone you trusted and shared intimacies with could also behave with duplicity may be impossible to fully accept. That is the aftereffect of predatory behavior.

Always remember: the emotional predator *recognizes emotions*—that is part of what makes him or her effective—but *experiences* only his or her own emotions. Hence, the person may possess a considerable emotional vocabulary and offer sound insights. But the predator *relates* only to what he or she goes through. This is why the person cannot see himself as a predator. The anger, sorrow, or need that they feel is their only emotive reality. This fuels a sense of rightness even as the predator acts in ways that may be ruthless. From the predatory perspective, all means are justified and rational.

Because this personality type is so prevalent, it may be, frankly, impossible to wholly avoid. You may find yourself dealing with short or long-term relationships with such figures at work, in families, in education, in the military, and so on. When you detect these relationships, do not blame yourself. But step around them carefully and separate as soon as you are able. This is easier done in institutional settings than in marriages or partnerships, of course, which may present long-term crises to solve.

But you will do better at any sort of relational crisis, and I write this from both success and failure, if you do not blame yourself. I am not a diagnostician. I am a longtime and fitful student on the road of life, and nothing else. From that, I estimate that these personas, as noted, makeup perhaps half of the population. Hence, the issue is not: "why did this happen to me?"—rather, it is likely that it *will at some point happen*. Growth occurs when you discover it. And when you do, take steps not to allow such abuse to repeat. If you are like me, this may entail several false starts. Again, do not engage in self-blame; just act.

Varieties of Predatory Experience

Emotionally predatory behavior can take so many different forms that it may appear innumerable in variety. But I will list the most prominent patterns, at least in my observation.

Subtle putdowns. Someone routinely drops rhetorical questions—"are you done with your Ph.D. yet?"—intended to subtly detract from your efforts or self-respect. The speaker often frames the statement in a manner that permits plausible denial of any intended offense. This *putdown / deniability* dynamic is, in fact, one of the giveaways of an emotional predator. If you detect this pattern, do not explain it away. Your awareness is a gift. Use it—and get away.

Insults. Someone references you, or your social circle / group, in a demeaning or diminishing way. For example, the person may not use a derogatory term to your face but will say something historically disparaging about a neighborhood, school, affiliation, or group to which you belong or identify. Again, this behavior harbors plausible denial, the key tool of the predator. In other cases, the party may be cordial in person but will use political or cultural slurs on social media. Predators sometimes conceal or excuse this by pretending victimhood themselves. Personally, I have never met a bully who did not self-identify as a victim, a point to watch for.

Obfuscation. Someone repeatedly allows deadlines to slip, resists specificity about figures or dates, leaves appointments or plans unconfirmed, does not acknowledge timely communications, or adopts a posture of remove at critical moments. Purposeful obscuration keeps you unsteady. It is a powerplay. Reject it.

Ersatz communication. The other party, perhaps upon learning that you are unhappy about something, agrees to talk through the issues, but actually uses drawn-out or murky exchanges as a tactic of exhaustion, manipulation, or information seeking for his or her own purposes. All of the talk, sometimes across hours, produces no change, and presents a drain on your time. As a friend put it: "Some people use communication as a way to block communication." It is a control ploy.

Reversals. The predatory party seemingly gives in, agrees with you, and vows a change—but summarily breaks his or her word. The person may agree in principle or vow to fix something on "Monday morning"—and never acts on it.

Undelivered gifts or promises. The person offers you some possibility in terms of a job, assignment, or invitation—and then drops it. Exchanges go silent or drift into noncommittal verbiage. This keeps you in a suspended state of wanting. It keeps you at their disposal.

Ghosting. Communication freeze-outs are common to our era but, like all facets of human nature, they predate the digital age. Social technology exacerbates longstanding human crises. Suppose someone initiates a relationship with you—and then drops you. Completely and without explanation. That is the ultimate predatory device. Once upon a time, a photographer shot images of me in a t-shirt (outside on a cold winter day) for her retail website. Without a cross word, she ghosted me and never shared the shots, wasting my time and causing me emotional confusion. When encountering such behavior, be glad, as I eventually was, that you avoided a worse entanglement. Nothing gives greater feelings of false power to the predator—filling a deficit that the person is unable to satisfy through relational or creative means—than attracting a new friend, collaborator, or confidant only to abruptly drop the person, thus creating bewilderment and hurt. Cruelty empowers the predator.

Get Out

When you discover an emotional predator, what step should you take? For one thing, do not confront the person. You will get nowhere. As noted, the predator always possesses, and will unfailingly use, plausible deniability. The confrontation will get turned against you ("you're too sensitive;" "you're overreacting;" "that's not what happened"), and you will become prey one more time. The chief thing is to acknowledge the truth to yourself and deftly but decisively—and permanently—separate.

These steps may not occur immediately. There may be ties and bonds that cannot be easily severed. But your inner acknowledgment is critical. Internal conviction possesses momentum of its own. Then, lay plans and silently act on them.

Some people feel unable to separate from a cruel antagonist due to family ties or financial needs. I sympathize with that—and offer this three-part approach:

1. Be certain that the bonds you feel are actual and not artificial. Fear of disapproval is not a valid excuse for remaining in proximity to a cruel person. Just because someone will disapprove of your decision is not a real bind. Every decision carries

consequences; the positive consequences of distancing from cruelty almost invariably outweigh the negative. Another person's judgment must not deter you. If it does, that is self-created.

2. If you have determined that you authentically wish to separate but are financially or otherwise bound, vow first to separate from the person internally. Acknowledge to yourself their cruelty and admit its grotesque and destructive nature. Never tell the other person what you are doing or thinking. Silently abide your insight. Remember: cruel people always have plausible denial. It is part of how they maintain their hold on you. Just knowing this makes you more powerful.

3. Vow to separate from the offender as a physical fact at the soonest possible opportunity. This opportunity will come, and probably sooner than you think. This is because effort sustains and fortifies growth. When you place yourself within the schema of effort, which these three steps are designed to do, opportunities for expansion and movement reach you. But the first and crucial step is determining that escape is what you really want.

Time Abided

I consider abolitionist hero Frederick Douglass (1818–1895) a voice of universal moral relevance. I want to recount a story from his life, which holds a critical lesson for people of every era and situation, even as it must also be understood within its historical context.

Born a slave in Maryland around 1818, Douglass was separated as a young child from his mother—a woman who walked miles from another plantation for the rare occasion of rocking him to sleep or giving him a handmade ginger cake. Douglass grew into a self-educated teen determined to escape north and never accept the role of complacency to a cruel overseer.

But, as Douglass recounted across all three of his memoirs,* in January 1834, on the eve of his sixteenth birthday, he found himself delivered into the hands of the worst of them, Edward Covey—known locally as "the breaker of Negroes."

A few years earlier, Douglass had been a domestic servant in Baltimore. There the burdens of slavery—the hunger, beatings, daily humiliations—were tempered by the surface civility of city life. The wife of his Baltimore household briefly taught him to read, until her husband abruptly ended the lessons. But Douglass discovered ways to keep building his literacy through whatever books or newspaper scraps could be found.

The Baltimore family soon rearranged its household, and Douglass was returned to plantation life. His new master in St. Michaels, Maryland, was suspicious: Could a teen who had tasted city life still work the fields? To be brutally certain, at the start of 1834 he "loaned out" Douglass for a year to Covey, a petty, cruel farmer who used every opportunity to beat his new charge on trumped-up offenses.

The beatings grew so severe that by August, Douglass snuck back to his old St. Michaels household to beg for protection. The youth, still bruised and caked with blood, was turned back to

---

* *Narrative of the Life of Frederick Douglass* (1845); *My Bondage and My Freedom* (1855); and *Life and Times of Frederick Douglass* (1893).

Covey's farm. Once there, Douglass hid all day and into the night in the woods outside Covey's fields, not knowing what to do.

To Covey's shock, Douglass did return to the farm. But when the beatings resumed, the youth stood up and fought back. For two hours one morning the two struggled, and Covey could not get the better of him. (I recount the full episode in my 2009 *Occult America*, where I focus on role played by the Black magickal tradition of hoodoo.)

Embarrassed by his inability to control a teenager who finally said *enough*, the slave master backed down. For Douglass, it was a moment of inner revolution from which he would never retreat. His act of self-defense, he wrote, freed him in mind and spirit, leaving him to await the opportunity to finally be free in body.

Even though Douglass repeatedly identified his resistance to Covey as the turning point of his life, it is important to note that he actually did not escape for more than four years. He made plans and was caught in 1836 and finally succeeded in September 1838 in fleeing from Baltimore to New York City.

But Douglass wrote that he was free in spirit the morning he asserted his own sense of personhood. I would never overextrapolate the narrative of a brutalized and enslaved person to the experience of most of us reading these words today in physical comfort and safety. That would be a grotesque misapplication. At the same time, however, a universal moral arc appears in Douglass's account, and I see him, in addition to being an abolitionist and memoirist, as an ethicist and philosopher.

If you have read carefully, you will detect my effort to encapsulate something of his narrative's lessons in the three points noted earlier. Again: in Douglass's life, escape required four years to emerge as physical fact.

No Sacred Cows

I want to describe how I advised a former neighbor in dealing with issues of cruelty. In 2012, Hurricane Sandy rocked New York City and many people lost power for days or weeks. (Curiously, the hoodoo practitioner who aided Frederick Douglass was also named Sandy.) A friend, whom I will call Carol, was stuck in a high-rise building with a young son who was suffering from a fever. She had no power, no elevator service, and could not leave the boy alone. Her husband was out of town.

She made arrangements to take the boy and stay with her mother-in-law and father-in-law, who lived in a luxury high-rise in a nearby suburb. They had full power. It seemed like a perfect and necessary solution. But as Carol told it—she is a mature person whose account I take seriously—her mother-in-law, with whom she'd had problems previously, was cruelly unwelcoming.

At every turn, the woman made Carol and her recuperating son feel unwelcome and intruding, even though Carol did her best to be a thoughtful guest. At one point Carol told her mother-in-law to please try and understand how difficult this situation was and how she needed a pinch of tolerance. "Well, this is no picnic for me either," was the woman's abrupt response.

Carol was deeply hurt by the experience. She recalled other times when her in-law had acted slighting or hostile. She was understandably upset. No stranger to therapy, spirituality, or self-help, she had tried for years to navigate and leaven the situation, but without success.

I told her: "Carol, have you considered that you could simply separate from this person? If her behavior is perpetually hostile, you could simply say no to holidays and other contacts. There may be consequences, but there are already consequences—you're in pain. Why be around her?"

She explained that she wanted her son to grow up within a family circle, and to have adults who could serve as role models and sources of dependability. I noted that her mother-in-law was neither of those things, and her son already had positive adults in his life.

I could see that she was energized by the prospect of an option. I did not feel it my business to push the point further. I do not think the separation ever occurred. But I wanted my friend to at least glimpse a broadened possibility. It is powerful simply to know that the choice exists and can always be renewed or revisited, however you go. The point is: you do not have to be around cruel people. There are consequences. In Carol's case, her husband presumably would have objected. But everything carries consequences. They are usually milder than imagined.

And benefits abound. Once you actually separate from cruelty, you will be amazed at how many other facets of your life improve. In many cases, you will rediscover yourself as a person of humor, even-temper, approachability, and steadiness. In that vein, I have been astonished to observe how many problems attributed to character, trauma, dysfunction, or over-sensitivity (a charge that cruel people almost always use to control you) suddenly lift once you are in the right company.

I believe that our therapeutic culture—positive as it has been in many ways—has inculcated many of us with the myth that our problems perpetually follow us unless we resolve psychological root causes or embrace correct "strategies." That is true in some cases. But in many cases I believe that children and adults are simply and egregiously misplaced. They are in the wrong kinds of company where they may feel bullied, misunderstood, or disdained. An altered setting can work dramatic changes, both personally and professionally.

I have been in settings where I had neighbors who were inconsiderate or hostile. Where my every effort at rapprochement ended disappointingly. I used to own a lake house in upstate New York. When I drove up and saw my neighbor's car in his driveway my stomach would tighten—and this was a place for relaxation!—because he perpetually encroached on my property with noise, errant fireworks, twenty-four-hour spotlights, crowds, a garish floating dock anchored in the middle of the lake, and a not-infrequent wisecrack. He was, in short, an asshole. No effort, from spiritual affirmations to personal appeals to a high fence made much difference.

There was one solution. Moving. When I finally moved I felt great. I had been in the wrong setting. I am mindful that moving or breaking ties is not always possible. I owned that house for fifteen years. I walked away at a loss. But I want you to understand that sometimes the only solution is using your feet.

If you absolutely cannot separate from someone at present, for reasons of economics, domesticity, or livelihood, revisit the story about Frederick Douglass. Swear silently that you will first separate from this person as a fact within—tell neither them nor anyone else of your vow—and you will free yourself as a physical fact at the soonest possible opportunity.

In the face of cruelty, most of us behave like sheep. But have you ever really observed sheep? One kick from a sheep can break a grown-man's ribs. Your kick is your escape.

Be Seen

I want to round out this chapter with focus on a subtler issue: refusing to linger in environments in which you are unseen.

In the early 1970s, my teacher was an idealistic member of the nascent Hare Krishna order, which had its first headquarters—still there—in a dingy little storefront in the East Village on First Avenue near Houston Street.

The HK movement was just getting started and they hadn't a stick of furniture inside. But what they did have was the guidance of Swami Prabhupada (1896–1977) whom my teacher, a man of real values and seriousness, said he considered a realized man, a term I never otherwise heard him use.

The Swami told his students that their first order of business was procuring or building benches. (The anarchist-Marxist collective at Stony Brook University used to call it "liberating" benches or whatever item was sought—but I don't think that's how the Swami meant it).

One day, Swami Prabhupada gave my friend a sacred Hindu book to borrow. Since there was no furniture in the place, he had nowhere to put it down. Not wanting to place it on the floor, he put it on top of his shoes by the door. My friend did yet realize that within traditional Hinduism shoes are considered very dirty and profane. When the Swami saw what he done he grew angry and told my teacher, "I see that you do not know how to properly treat a scared book—return it to me at once!"

My friend told me: "I realized at that moment that this man could not be my teacher. Because he could not see me."

My friend would never disrespect a hallowed book. Never. That the Swami could not see that meant that my friend would have to leave and find a guide elsewhere. He soon grew dedicated to the Gurdjieff work, where I knew him.

Ironically—although I think purposefully—this cycle repeated in our lives. It may be intrinsic to the teacher-student relationship. My love for him has never once flagged.

In any case, the lesson I take from his story is this: you must never compromise your sense of self on the path. If a "realized" person (I have never met one) misjudges you, act on that knowledge. The path requires hardy travelers not cowering rabbits.

The path also requires people with sufficient intellect not to have to show off how smart or in-the-know they are. Let someone else be smart. But never relinquish your being.

There is an expression: *when the student is ready, the teacher appears.* I believe that the reverse must also be true. Protect yourself in the search and in all environments.

I once prayed for wisdom. Wisdom is experience. I received experience. I write this chapter from no other place. If what I observe matches your inner sensibility, use it.

CHAPTER SIX

Why "Never Give Up" Is a Metaphysical Law

Napoleon Hill repeatedly emphasizes perseverance. Next to a Definite Chief Aim (DCA), "sticking to it" is the central theme of his program. Aside from the apparently commonsensical nature of his advice, what backs it?

I consider perseverance lawful. It is the single best guarantor, barring extreme countervailing conditions (which do exist), of personal deliverance. I received this insight from the work of twentieth-century spiritual philosopher G.I. Gurdjieff (1866–1949). Gurdjieff constantly pushed his students to surpass their limits of perceived strength.

In his posthumous memoir, *Meetings with Remarkable Men*, first published in English in 1963, the teacher recalled episodes from when he and a band of followers fled civil war-torn Russia. In an epilogue, "The Material Question," he addressed their desperate need for money.

In the summer of 1922, following a dangerous flight across Eastern Europe, Gurdjieff and his students reached Paris with razor-thin resources. Procuring an old estate, the Prieuré, to function as living quarters and school, Gurdjieff used every means possible to ensure his circle's financial survival.

"The work went well," he wrote, "but the excessive pressure of these months, immediately following eight years of uninterrupted labours, fatigued me to such a point that my health was severely shaken, and despite all my desire and effort I could no longer maintain the same intensity."

Seeking to restore his strength through a dramatic change in setting as well as fundraise for the institute, Gurdjieff devised a plan to tour America with forty-six students. The troupe would put on demonstrations of the sacred dances they practiced and present Gurdjieff's lectures and ideas to the public. Although intended to attract donors, the ocean voyage and lodgings entailed significant upfront expenses. Last-minute adjustments and unforeseen costs consumed nearly all the teacher's remaining resources.

"To set out on such a long journey with such a number of people," he wrote, "and not have any reserve cash for an emergency was, of course, unthinkable." The trip itself, so meticulously prepped and planned for, faced collapse.

"And then," Gurdjieff wrote, "as has happened to me more than once in critical moments of my life, there occurred an entirely unexpected event." He continued:

> What occurred was one of those interventions that people who are capable of thinking consciously—in our times and particularly in past epochs—have always considered a sign of the just providence of the Higher Powers. As for me, I would say that it was *the law-conformable result of a man's unflinching perseverance in bringing all his manifestations into accordance with the principles he has consciously set himself in life for the attainment of a definite aim.* [emphasis added]

As Gurdjieff sat in his room pondering their troubles, his elderly mother entered. She had reached Paris just a few days earlier. His mother was part of the group fleeing Russia but she and others got stranded in the Caucasus. "It was only recently that I had succeeded," Gurdjieff wrote, "after a great deal of trouble, in getting them to France."

She handed her son a package, which she told him was a burden from which she desperately wished to be relieved. Gurdjieff opened the package to discover a forgotten brooch of significant value that he had given her back in Eastern Europe. He intended it as a barter item to pass a border or secure food and shelter. He assumed it was long since sold or otherwise traded and never again thought of it. But there it was. At the precipice of ruin, they were saved.

"I almost jumped up and danced for joy," he wrote. This was the lawful result of "unflinching perseverance." As with all Gurdjieff wrote and said, there is at the back of his statement a level of gravitas and lived experience that makes this teaching warranting of deep pause. Things that might appear homiletic in the mouth of a lesser figure took on life-and-death seriousness from this teacher.

I suspect a metaphysical underpinning to Gurdjieff's story that contains two (though not only two) prospects: 1) our concept of linear time is illusory, and 2) because of the first, what appears lost can be gained; what appears settled is anything but.

No Regrets

We often rue the 20/20 nature of hindsight as though it provides no payoff beyond melancholic wisdom of what could have been. But time, rather than an arrow moving in a sole direction as classical physics dictates, is, in fact, a matrix of infinitude through which we may, and always do, step in any direction via measurement, perception, observation, and continuance of effort after presumed fact.

Keep in mind that "feeling" something—such as personal independence or, for that matter, the earth's motion, proves a poor guide to actuality. Writing in his second epilogue to *War and Peace*—in the concluding lines of the work itself—Leo Tolstoy (1828–1910) noted humanity's earlier necessity of acknowledging heliocentrism to save itself from absurdity, which he compared to modern man's psychological predicament:

> In the first case it was necessary to renounce the consciousness of an unreal immobility in space and to recognize a motion we did not feel; in the present case it is similarly necessary to renounce a freedom that does not exist, and to recognize a dependence of which we are not conscious.

I believe that Western culture occupies a similar position today, more than a century after Tolstoy's death. In order to save ourselves from absurdity, there must soon come acknowledgment of nonlocal and extraphysical aspects of existence and with it acknowledgment that time is not the restrictive linearity it appears.

"Cycles," said esoteric Egyptologist R. A. Schwaller de Lubicz (1887–1961), "are the only way to beat time and space. Yes, the only way to beat those two is on their own ground. And cyclical consciousness places it there. Time is not like a river that flows by and in which you cannot step twice. Time is a spiral, and space as well, a spherical spiral. Can you imagine a spherical spiral? Try!"

Schwaller's point is further suggested by the Tao Te Ching, in a passage at once familiar and elusive: timing is everything. Likewise, the symbol of the ouroboros or spherical serpent biting its tail. And the cyclicality of the I Ching (itself an esoteric time keeping device) as well as the Mayan Long-Count calendar.

I quote Schwaller from the extraordinary 1987 memoir *Al-Kemi: Hermetic, Occult, Political, and Private Dimensions of R.A. Schwaller de Lubicz* by André Vanden Broeck. I encountered this book in 2005 at a transition in my life. It fortified my conviction that occultism, at its subtlest, is intellectually sound. I was not always certain. In his 1947 essay, "Theses Against Occultism," Frankfurt School philosopher Theodor W. Adorno wrote, "Occultism is the metaphysic of dunces." He was wrong—yet he opened me to an idea that has expanded despite not being dwelt on: how intellectuals I admired growing up were, like the most ordinary minds, locked into judging category of query versus scale of quality.

I reencountered *Al-Kemi* nearly twenty years later and the day before my fifty-ninth birthday; the book evokes strange memories filled with vulnerability. Its mysterious author, Vanden Broeck, was then living in retirement at a hotel in Mexico managed by his son. His publisher gave me his fax number. "I do not participate in the internet," Vanden Broeck wrote me. He sent a friendly fax in response to my initial outreach noting that he used to live on New York's Hudson Street where my publishing company was then located. Thereafter he went silent. I had the impression, perhaps retrocausal in nature, that he did not wish me to write an expository appreciation of his book. His publisher, too, previously friendly, went silent. My path is not theirs. It is one of exposition.

Ancient logic is splitting one to get two. Modern logic is adding one to get two. Exposition is not l'expérience (which can also mean experiment) but, as Schwaller observed, it is next best.

"The reason for this lack of contact," André wrote in *Al-Kemi*, "holds no mystery: he [Schwaller] did not believe in language. Yet it is through language, both his and mine, that I discovered him."

This chapter attempts—with clinical data of its own—to offer the language of Schwaller's ineffable truth of time as "spherical spiral" versus progressing line. It is my effort to drag the ineffable into what literary critic Irving Howe—another intellectual hero growing up—in his 1986 *The American Newness* called "the shallows of the explicit." That is the job I have assumed. It was offered and I accepted it.

Backwards Causation

The rational world we know quietly changed in 2011. This change came at the hands of Cornell psychologist Daryl J. Bem. The parapsychologist Bem is the reverse-image of the founder of pseudo-skepticism, stage magician and MacArthur fellow James Randi (1928–2020). Both men grew up Jewish-misfit-boy magicians. Following a childhood of humiliation by bullies—forcing Daryl's Denver family to move homes—he, like James, took refuge in stage magic. But unlike the faux-skeptic, the grown Bem determined not to bleed the world of mystery but to study its contours.

After a long and distinguished research career, Bem suffered unprecedented professional and media evisceration when his 2011 paper in a scholarly journal detailed a decade of clinical evidence for precognition and retrocausality, in which future events cognitively impact present ones.* Bem seemed fated to repeat his

---

* "Feeling the Future: Experimental Evidence for Anomalous Retroactive Influences on Cognition and Affect" by Daryl J. Bem, *Journal of Personality and Social Psychology*, 2011, Vol. 100, No. 3

early years, now at the hands of *media bullies*, from *Slate* to the *New York Times*, who, absent evidence and ignoring their critics (like me), deemed him the poster child for bad science. Their logic? The unfalsifiable hypothesis that precognition cannot exist because precognition cannot exist.

A decade on, however, the unthinkable occurred: Bem's findings were widely replicated and proven confirmatory in a large-scale meta-analysis.* His work is physics-meets-alchemy as evidence demonstrates that actions you take in the future affect the present. Just as Einstein, Schrödinger, and innumerable mystics taught: 1) time is not linear, and 2) all events are infinite at once. Professional skeptics, like a clunky Soviet bureaucracy, endure; but in 2011 the dialectics (if I may) of immateriality turned: realities of interdimensionality, psi, and humanity's ineffable existence are the genie that cannot be rebottled.

Here are basics. For about ten years prior to publication, Bem conducted a series of nine experiments involving more than 1,000 participants into precognition or "time reversing" of widely established cognitive or psychological effects, such as memorization of a list or predicting / responding to negative or erotic stimuli flashed as images on a screen. Bem's discoveries demonstrated the reach of cognition across boundaries of linear time.

Bem, as with other researchers, including Dean Radin of the Institute of Noetic Sciences (IONS), identified factors that seem to correlate with precognition, such as the body's response to arousing or disturbing imagery. As Bem wrote of previous

---

* "REVISED: Feeling the future: A meta-analysis of 90 experiments on the anomalous anticipation of random future events" [version 2; peer review: 2 approved] by Daryl Bem, Patrizio E. Tressoldi, Thomas Rabeyron, Michael Duggan, first published: 30 Oct 2015, latest published: 29 Jan 2016, last updated: 23 Jul 2020, *F1000Research*

experiments in presentiment of stimuli: "Most of the pictures were emotionally neutral, but a highly arousing negative or erotic image was displayed on randomly selected trials. As expected, strong emotional arousal occurred when these images appeared on the screen, but the remarkable finding is that the increased arousal was observed to occur a few seconds before the picture appeared, before the computer had even selected the picture to be displayed."

In one of Bem's trials, subjects were asked to "guess" at random erotic images alternated with benign images. "Across all 100 sessions," he wrote, "participants correctly identified the future position of the erotic pictures significantly more frequently than the 50% hit rate expected by chance: 53.1%... In contrast, their hit rate on the nonerotic pictures did not differ significantly from chance: 49.8%... This was true across all types of nonerotic pictures: neutral pictures, 49.6%; negative pictures, 51.3%; positive pictures, 49.4%; and romantic but nonerotic pictures, 50.2%." You will note the slender but statistically significant effect referenced here, which is typical of parapsychology experiments. The measurable impact is not like Zeus throwing lightning bolts at earth but rather a detectable "signal in the noise," which requires precise measurement and circumstantial cultivation.

Bem's horizons, however, extended further. In the most innovative aspect of his nine-part study, the researcher set out to discover, in experiments eight and nine, whether subjects displayed improved recall of lists of words that were to be practice-memorized in the future:

> Inspired by the White Queen's claim, the current experiment tested the hypothesis that memory can "work both ways" by testing whether rehearsing a set of words

makes them easier to recall—even if the rehearsal takes place after the recall test is given. Participants were first shown a set of words and given a free recall test of those words. They were then given a set of practice exercises on a randomly selected subset of those words. The psi hypothesis was that the practice exercises would retroactively facilitate the recall of those words, and, hence, participants would recall more of the to-be-practiced words than the unpracticed words.

Bem found a statistically significant improvement of recall on the lists of words studied in the near future: "The results show that practicing a set of words after the recall test does, in fact, reach back in time to facilitate the recall of those words."

In experiment nine, this retroactive effect heightened when researchers added a refined practice exercise. ("A new practice exercise was introduced immediately following the recall test in an attempt to further enhance the recall of the practice words. This exercise duplicated the original presentation of each word that participants saw prior to the recall test, but only the practice words were presented.") The results improved: "This modified replication yielded an even stronger psi effect than that in the original experiment." In general, future memorization heightened current recall.

Within a year of Bem's publication, a trio of professional skeptics published a rejoinder. Playing off of Bem's "Feeling the Future," their paper sported the media-friendly title, "Failing the Future."* The skeptics reran Bem's ninth experiment. They

---

* "Failing the Future: Three Unsuccessful Attempts to Replicate Bem's 'Retroactive Facilitation of Recall' Effect" by Stuart J. Ritchie, Richard Wiseman, Christopher C. French, *PLoS ONE*, March 2012, Volume 7, Issue 3

wrote in their abstract: "Nine recently reported parapsychological experiments appear to support the existence of precognition. We describe three pre-registered independent attempts to exactly replicate one of these experiments, 'retroactive facilitation of recall', which examines whether performance on a memory test can be influenced by a post-test exercise. All three replication attempts failed to produce significant effects... and thus do not support the existence of psychic ability."

The authors omitted a critical detail from their own database. By deadline, they possessed two independent studies that replicated Bem's results. They made no mention of the opposing studies despite their preset ground rules for doing so.

As even his critics noted, Bem opened his database and software and provided instruction manuals free to anyone who wished to rerun his experiments. As of July 2020, Bem's experiments (including the original trials) showed replication in a meta-analysis encompassing ninety experiments in thirty-three laboratories in fourteen countries. "To encourage replications," Bem and his coauthors wrote in the abstract of their follow-up paper, "all materials needed to conduct them were made available on request. We here report a meta-analysis of 90 experiments from 33 laboratories in 14 countries which yielded an overall effect... greatly exceeding" the standard for "'decisive evidence' in support of the experimental hypothesis."

Scholar of Western esotericism Richard Kaczynski further clarifies the matter in his impeccable 2025 study *Mind Over Magick*:

> Bem and colleagues subsequently published a meta-analysis of ninety replications of his research, taking place in thirty-three laboratories in fourteen countries,

resulting in the calculation of a small but significant effect size of 0.09. In statistics, effect sizes are often classed as small (0.30), medium (0.50), and large (0.70). Thus, the effect of psi is quite small, but statistically significant: $p = 1.2 \times 10^{-10}$ (in other words, the odds of the results from so many studies falling this far from zero due to chance alone is one in 8 billion).*

Use It

I offer two anecdotes that suggest potential uses of backwards causation.

Recent to this writing, I heard from a professional Thai kickboxer, Spencer Hanley. Spencer's fights appear all over digital media. At the time, he was training for a match outside Houston, Texas. He had nine days before the bout and wrote seeking advice on sharpening his mental game. Spencer felt good about his training but needed guidance to stay "on" mentally.

---

* Because I want constructive skeptics and general readers to have an idea of the effortful and earnest "number crunching" in parapsychology, I am reproducing verbatim an email exchange of May 27, 2025, with the author:

"Richard, I am very interested in Daryl Bem's work and highlighted this graph of your excellent book...

Are these 1 / 8 billion odds based on the confirmatory studies (i.e., 18 out of 90); the P-value; or an overall aggregate of the confirmatory / non confirmatory studies in the sample? Or something else? Thank you!! -M-"

"Hi Mitch, The "one in 8 billion" figure comes from the p-value: It's the inverse of p=1.2 x 10^-10 = 8.3333 x 10^9.

I rounded to 8 billion because when you're dealing with numbers that small (or, inversely, large), we don't have many significant digits to work with. What follows the 2 in 1.2 can change the answer quite a bit in the hundreds of millions,but that first digit, 8, is definite. All best, Richard"

I suggested a simple exercise called the 30-Day Mental Challenge. It appears in Appendix C. The challenge requires writing and signing a contract committing you for thirty days to directing your thoughts along progressive, positive, and productive lines. Spencer said he would do it. But his fight was only nine days away. He needed something more immediate. This *is* immediate, I explained. A trick appears in this exercise that allows you "to beat time and space." And I guaranteed him that no one in the opposing corner was even thinking about it.

In short, I continued, there exists an entirely real prospect that what you do in the future, i.e., following a given event, may improve your cognition and performance during the event itself. Referencing Bem's study, I noted that the clinician supplied recent, juried, and replicated data to support a retrocausal effect in cognition. As demonstrated in his lab experiments—and confirmed in largescale meta-analysis—future actions benefit present cognition. This is "impossible" insofar as super-position is impossible; particles (e.g., positrons) traveling backwards in time is impossible; surpassing lightspeed (e.g., quantum entanglement) is impossible; and, of course, ESP, so widely validated in bulletproof data, is impossible. If we eliminated everything that classical and Newtonian physics (if not Newton himself) deems impossible, we would erase world-class science, including quantum computing.

It must be noted that Bem's trials focused exclusively on cognition. I consider it a reasonable experiment (or *l'expérience*) to seek similar benefit in physical or athletic ability. Plus, Spencer was seeking help with his mental-emotional preparedness, which is not unrelated to cognition. In any case, tendrils of connection are not strictly linear and experiments with retrocausality may evince results that violate standard perceptions of past, present, and future. Spencer vowed to try.

He won the fight. He dominated the match and appeared relaxed, good natured, and respectful toward his foe. Of course, he might have won anyway. But I like this wrinkle: for his entry song, rather than the usual death metal or drill rap many fighters choose, Spencer selected the pop classic "Heaven Is a Place on Earth." One of the ringside announcers said: "The fact that he's coming out to Belinda Carlisle makes me so happy." Several weeks after the match, and before my writing about it, I received DM voicemails from someone I had never met or followed: singer-songwriter Belinda Carlisle. Other than a high-school crush (Jones Beach Theater on Long Island, summer of '82) and enduring love for her music, I had no currency with the artist. In two detailed and thoughtful messages, she said she was reading my books and was a fan. Dying happy in 3, 2, 1...

More recently, a friend wrote to say she was applying for a deeply needed and desired job at a New York City religious organization. She recounted:

> I was on unemployment insurance and stressed TF out on a real first chakra level, the whole thing being on the same wavelength as shit I've been dredging and clearing for WAY too long... When I had that thought about the job, it felt like "that's for me." Or more like "I WANT THAT," with maybe a twinge of "Why can't I have that?"

In short, she was hopeful but nervous. Time passed and for some reason the job went to another person. She felt despondent. I offered the same basic advice given to Spencer with the wrinkle that she continue to hone her skills and presentation, and actively burnish her qualifications for the position. (She also gamely applied for other openings.) If it did not help, certainly it could not hurt. She agreed.

About a week later, she wrote me ecstatic. The boss "emailed me again and said that he had what he hoped was good news. It was the same job but with more hours. Amazing Grace Attack!!"

Pruning Shears

This episode calls to mind an exercise prescribed by Neville Goddard, "the pruning shears of revision." Neville advised revising a regretful event by imaginatively reliving it "from the end" of how you would like it to have gone. Hence, a disappointing encounter could be transformed into a positive one through entering and experiencing the "feeling state" and imaginative scene of a happy outcome.

Assuming the efficacy of Neville's method, and in light of the factors I have cited, what is actually occurring? What if the antecedent event and its alternative each proceed in real but different dimensions? Your alteration forms or perceives another dimensional strand or string—try to imagine reality as an endlessly and concentrically expanding ball of twine—with the "anchor strand" from which you first experienced the event circumstantially untouched. Perhaps your perception "leaps" to or weaves another strand, every bit as real and contextual as the anchor strand. This occurs without upending your sense of self, history, or location because it is as real as the other outcome. But it is now localized and experienced by you as solid, solitary, and unchanging. You may no longer recall the negative event.

Another possibility is that what is touched, what is altered, is the emotional antecedent of the event. So that your anchor reality and the psyches of those you encounter within it—independent beings who crisscross within your perception of reality or intertwined strings, as you do within theirs—are leavened by alteration of experience even though the forensics may be unchanged. Hence, if you consider a piece of evidence from the past, like an email, it may reflect the same incident, i.e., current reality evinces the same empirical markings. But because you wove or identified a new strand—you selected a different dimensional storyline and thus launched another among infinite timelines—there may exist a reverberation in which salving qualities either appear or are felt at the anchor point. (There is also, by this logic, another reality—one among an infinite number—where altered circumstance, either jarring or salving, is, in fact, experienced.) Within the reality of your inceptive thought point, the emotive ripple is felt. Healing can occur. The opposite is also true, so we must be careful when we consider the question of changing our past or when we idly revise, rerun, or reinforce scenes.

From the perspective of the figures in the famous Schrödinger's Cat thought experiment—the observer and the cat—they are singular, local, and concrete. But quantum laws dictate that this is only a point of view. In actuality, these figures, beyond their personal perspective, are multi-dimensional. So are you and me.

Neville equated revision with forgiveness. In his mystical reading of Scripture, to forgive does not mean to excuse but to re-vision an adversary or a fractious encounter according to your ideal. I am not always emotionally or ethically certain that I want to undo or reverse an event so much as resolve it on my own terms. This is a fact of human nature with which we must honestly reckon. Do you want peace—or victory? Is one exclusive of the other? Our emotions always pull in the direction of authentic desire. Our inner or outer voices often conceal our motives; our emotions expose them.

I believe that there exist times when we actually *want* to retain negative situations, themes, or memories. For example, a perceived adversary may be someone for whom you harbor deep feelings, even love. What is love but the opposing polarity of hate? In both situations, another person shapes, marks, and even gives direction or purpose to your life. Love and hate are, in a sense, the same rhythmical and emotional continuum.

Relatedly, we may wish, without acknowledging it to ourselves, to retain, review, and even re-live a difficulty. That dynamic may also occur because the disturbing episode afforded us no emotional closure so we continually rerun it in search of resolve. Closure is a subjective feeling that arises from exiting a situation with some personally conceived degree of dignity, approval, or maturity. It is a restoration of self, objectively accurate or not.

Other times, you may savor conflict, which might provide a feeling of aliveness or even a thrill of having escaped. Such an attachment could present myriad or conflicting emotions. Fear and allure are also part of the same continuum. Finally, a trauma cycle may evoke feelings of injustice, which you fitfully, and often unconvincingly, use your imagination to fix or restore. This can lead to "what ifs?" in which you reimagine telling someone off or rescuing yourself from trouble through foresight or a quick response.

None of what I just described is revision in the manner defined by Neville. But nor am I exactly criticizing these approaches either. A wise man once said that justice is nothing but a mental idea, i.e., a necessarily limited or peripherally blind perspective based on selfishness or perceptual boundaries. I have abided his statement for years. I am unsure it is true, at least as an absolute. I believe that the mature individual possesses a valid scale of reference for how he or she is treated in life, and likewise has some conception of just and unjust scenarios pertaining to autonomy of psyche and body as well as ethical standards.

From the perspective of larger currents of reciprocity, an event may satisfy one's thirst for justice, albeit indirectly. This may be what Nietzsche had in mind when he wrote in *Beyond Good and Evil* in 1886: "One *has* to repay good and ill—but why precisely to the person who has done us good or ill?" (From Walter Kaufmann's 1966 translation.) This is a disquieting principle. Why should payment be extracted from an uninvolved pedestrian? To this objection the philosopher might reply: Why then should good tidings be granted to any such person?—as in the popular concept of "pay it forward." Perhaps both consequences are unwarranted on an intimate scale but arise from matters beyond our perception. Nietzsche's ideal may reflect the impersonal scales of life found within concepts of karma in Vedic theology.

In traditional Hinduism and Buddhism, karmic balances of equilibrium are unseeable, ineffable, not infrequently harsh, and occur across vast reaches of time. In that vein, I might reframe Nietzsche's statement from "one has to repay" to "nature has to repay." Both Nietzsche and the wise man I quoted earlier remind me that I must bow to limits of perspective. That said, I will venture this: When someone humiliates you, consider that it may be retrocausal from what that person is going to suffer. Time is a "spherical spiral."

What I can conclude is that the effectiveness of Neville's pruning-shears approach rests upon the authenticity and emotional clarity of the individual's wish to undo knots. This is why, again and again, I emphasize self-honesty. It is the solution upon which every choice and possibility rests, at least insofar as we can be said to function independently.

Time Travel?

In season six of *Better Call Saul*, Walter White calls a "time machine" both a "real and theoretical impossibility." His "theoretical impossibility" is based on the second law of thermodynamics. According to this law, backwards movement in time is a virtual impossibility. This is because molecules placed into an agitated state, or heat, cannot of themselves return to their previously static state. Just as Humpty Dumpty does not reassemble, entropy does not reverse.

But this conclusion must be viewed through the lenses of both classical and quantum physics, as well as understood for its subtlety. As author L.D. Deutsch notes in her pristine 2025 study *Time, Myth, and Matter*: "Einstein's theory of special relativity does imply that all moments in time exist in some permanent location along the temporal dimension of the block universe." (I cannot say enough to recommend Deutsch's book: if I were a hiring manager, I would require every employee to read it so they would know what reality is.)

When referring to "time" we are referencing measurement of time versus the thing itself (whatever it may be); likewise we reference the unitary "arrow of time"—itself a measurement concept—to explain the near-impossibility of unbreaking an egg (again, the second law of thermodynamics). But time is more unruly and fantastical, as seen within quantum versus classical physics; Einstein considered the quantum field open ended or at least incomplete.

A series of conferences, "Quantum Retrocausation," convened by the University of San Diego (USD) and American Association for the Advancement of Science (AAAS) have been exploring the question of time reversal and retrocausality. As of this writing, papers from the latest in 2017 are collected in the American Institute of Physics (AIP) Conference Proceedings volume 1841, issue 1.* The preface by USD physics professor Daniel Sheehan notes:

> Quantum Retrocausation III is the third in a series of international symposia convened at the University of San Diego under the auspices of the Pacific Division of the American Association for the Advancement of Science (AAAS), to discuss the intersection of time and consciousness... Its focus was on a specific aspect of time—retrocausation—because it is here that time and consciousness intersect to beget several of the most compelling experimental mysteries and theoretical puzzles in physics.
>
> Retrocausation is the proposition that the future can affect the present in a manner analogous to how the past affects the present via causation. It is well known that the fundamental equations of physics are time-symmetric—that is, they possess time-forward (retarded) and time-reversed (advanced) solutions—yet this belies our temporally asymmetric experience of the world, which progresses unidirectionally toward the future. Physics almost universally adopts this prejudice by discarding advanced solutions as "unphysical". This symposium challenges this assumption.
>
> Various "arrows of time" have been recognized by physics for more than a century... These presume solely causation, thus precluding retrocausation. This is understandable insofar as the former helps provide the narrative structure consonant with our experience

---

* The table of contents appears here: https://pubs.aip.org/aip/acp/issue/1841/1

and physical theories; however, causation itself—and, by extension, retrocausation—has been philosophically suspect since at least the time of Hume. Causes are invisible, they are inferred from events but are not intrinsic to them; correlations, by contrast, can be directly measured. Causes are reasons given to well-established correlations, signposts for the stories we tell to make sense of the world and physical theory. Thus, retrocausation may be as illusory as causation—and perhaps just as necessary.

In QRC-III retrocausation was discussed within the context of quantum mechanics, a subject, not coincidentally, also largely defined through correlations, puzzles and paradoxes, e.g., Einstein's bubble, Schrödinger's cat, EPR, Wigner's friend, Wheeler's delayed choice, quantum eraser, interaction free measurements, and many others. While this list bespeaks the depth and richness of the field, it also evidences its theoretic incompleteness; after all, paradoxes are the seeds of truth, not its fruit.

This query seems to me the most exciting facet of natural philosophy today—and the springboard for a new era in understanding. Again, as Sheehan notes, "paradoxes are the seeds of truth, not its fruit."

"Neville, I can't quite go along with you..."

In considering this material, I am further struck by the prescience of Neville Goddard's ideas. In one of the final lectures of his life, delivered April 3, 1972 (he died October 1, 1972), the mystic recounted a remarkable story from 1949, which, as is often the case with Neville's accounts, bears the marking of truth. It elucidates the core of this query.

> I'll go back now to 1949. I was in Milwaukee, and I gave a series of lectures on the Bible. And this couple, he was a physicist, the head physicist, of Allis-Chalmers. They're a huge, big manufacturing firm making these turbines, sometimes bigger than this interior, and he was the head of the chemical department, where they would send waters from all over the world, who bought the turbine, and he would analyze the water to discover the problem that they faced; because the water, as it came through the stream, gathered the chemicals, and then the chemicals deposited itself within the turbine; and so they would send him samples of the water, and then he would analyze the water, and then send them the solution to their problem.
>
> Well, being a trained chemist, and the head of the department, he didn't take issue with me, but he said: "Neville, I can't quite go along with you because as a chemist, it's in conflict with my training. You tell me that I can go forward in time, that you can move backward in time, that all things are, and everything is now, at this very moment. And yet you are telling me that you can make things change, and it is in conflict with my training." We have a law known, said he, and we call it entropy. And entropy means that the past is fixed and unalterable. You cannot change it. If that could be changed, it throws everything out of kilter in my lab. I must know the past is unalterable, like braiding a lady's

hair, and the braided part, that's fixed. The rest is the future, not yet braided. We are waiting to see how it will develop from the braided part because that is completely fixed and unalterable. And you tell me it is not; that the whole vast world exists now, past, present, and future, and that you can go into these sections of time, in a world that is finished. Well, I can't go along with that.

That's perfectly all right. I'm not a chemist; I'm not a scientist, so I cannot argue the point with you. I only know my visions. And I teach vision as I have actually experienced it. And I can go into these spots. I have gone into these places and the past has not passed away. And it's fixed, as you say, but I'm quite sure one could go back and revise that past and change it. And I can go forward into the future that I do know and set it up to walk across a bridge of incident; when I come to that point in time where I have entered, it takes on the color, the tone, and the reality that I assumed it to be when I entered that state.

Can't be done. But he was a very honest man, as most of these fellows are; they're trained to be honest. How else could they achieve what they do achieve in science unless they're perfectly honest with themselves?

Well, in the month of November, I received a letter from him and he sent me the science newsletter dated October the 15th. And it was all about the positron. And the one who wrote it was Professor Richard Feynman, he was then a professor of physics at Cornell University. Twenty years later, only last year, they granted him the Nobel Prize in physics for that paper.* It took them twenty years to recognize what he said as theory back in 1949. And if I can quote it, this is it: "The positron is a wrong-way electron. It's 'wrong way' in every sense of the word. It moves backward in time. It moves from where it hasn't been and speeds to where it was an instant ago. Arriving there, it is bumped so hard its time-sense is reversed and it moves back to where it hasn't been."

Now that is not Neville speaking; that is Professor Feynman. For that, he got the Nobel Prize last year. He said: "It's not only backward in that sense, but even its charge is backward. It's a positron; it's positive and not negative. And yet it is an electron."**

When they first observed it or rather had it as theory, they did not want to admit it, but yet it fitted in with Einstein's theory, mathematically, so they had to in some way accept it, but no one had ever photographed it. Then came someone who photographed it in their studies of the cosmic rays, and here it was the actual positron. It seemed as though two were developed at a certain point. And it wasn't, said he. That

---

* The paper to which Neville accurately refers is, "The Theory of Positrons" by R.P. Feynman, *Physical Review*, Volume 76, Number 6, September 15, 1949. In 1965, Feynman received the Nobel Prize for physics, shared with Julian Schwinger and Shin'ichirō Tomonaga, for their "fundamental work in quantum electrodynamics, with deep-ploughing consequences for the physics of elementary particles." Neville's talk appears in the anthology *Neville Goddard's Final Lectures* (G&D Media, 2022), which I edited and introduced.

** Electrons carry a negative charge.

one coming back, which was the positron, should, if it is bounced, it should be deflected and continue on its course, but deflected course. On the other hand, if it's bounced so hard, it's not deflected; it's reversed and moves forward in a normal manner to where it hasn't been.

Well, I told him that I was sitting at home, and I would go into a section of time, even this year, for instance. This is now only April. I put myself in Christmas. I would feel the stores are all dressed for Christmas. I could hear the music of Christmas, all the carols. I'd walk through Saks Fifth Avenue in New York City, go into Best, go into the other, and I would feel all that I would feel if it were true that it's Christmas, that it's the month of Christmas. And then when I feel that it's all Christmas, then I would feel that things are as I desire them to be back in the month, say, of March or July, which was certainly not Christmas season. So, take a hot, hot day in July, and I'm feeling it to be cold, and snow on the ground, and all the dressings for Christmas. And then I would open my eyes, and bounce back, and shock myself because it seems so real to me that, when I came back and opened my eyes upon July, and it's hot, I thought, now, are you kidding yourself? No, when I went forward in time quite normally, waiting out the days, the months to the month of December, things happened as I actually had assumed that they would. I went forward and determined, predetermined, what would happen.

WHY "NEVER GIVE UP" IS A METAPHYSICAL LAW

Well, when he sent me this, he wrote a sweet, lovely letter saying, Neville, I must confess: I didn't see it; no one saw it until Professor Feynman in his lab discovered this. But he discovered it by theory, and you tell me you know it by vision. You're not a scientist, and yet all that you said to me—which I could not believe, and even this moment it's difficult for me to believe, here comes the great professor, a theoretical physicist, and he is the one who wrote this paper. For that, he got the Nobel Prize last year. He worked on our atomic bomb; he worked on the hydrogen bomb. Then he asked the government to relieve him of the secrecy imposed upon him because of his position, and he came here to Caltech and taught at Caltech: theoretical physics. He said I want the freedom of imagination. I didn't want to be confined with the secrets of government so that I could not express myself. Leave me alone, all in theory. So, he goes blindly on with his mathematics and his theory, bringing out these concepts, all theory. Well, mine is not theory.

As a further matter of testimony—this time yours—does retrocausality or backwards causation really work? You already possess evidence that it does. The exploration you just finished reading is a product of it. When I began this passage, I worried about having sufficient time to complete it satisfactorily, to plumb the possibilities, to refine its ideas. It occurred to me: continue after the fact; invest the written exploration with its claim in action. You can judge the result.

Afterword

On May 14, 2025, I heard from a thoughtfully skeptical reader who challenged the Bem experiments. Our verbatim exchange follows:

Robin Doermann
May 14

The best attempt to replicate these results, found here, https://royalsocietypublishing.org/doi/10.1098/rsos.191375, was unable to do so.

From the article here https://www.skeptic.org.uk/2023/03/the-transparent-psi-project-the-results-are-in-so-where-are-all-the-headlines/:

This study was carried out Zoltan Kekecs of Lund University and a large international team of collaborators (there are no less that 30 co-authors on their paper recently published in Royal Society Open Science). The results pretty conclusively demonstrate that the technique used in the original experiment is not capable of demonstrating precognition, if indeed precognition really exists. Strangely, I have yet to see any reports in the media of this negative finding.

The plain word summary presented in the paper is worth quoting in full:

"This project aimed to demonstrate the use of research methods designed to improve the reliability of scientific findings in psychological science. Using this rigorous methodology, we could not replicate the positive findings of Bem's 2011 Experiment 1. This finding does not confirm, nor contradict the existence of ESP in general, and this was not the point of our study. Instead, the results tell us that (1) the original experiment was likely affected by methodological flaws or it was a chance finding, and (2) the paradigm used in the original study is probably not useful for detecting ESP effects if they exist. The methodological innovations implemented in this study enable the readers to trust and verify our results which is an important step forward in achieving trustworthy science."

Mitch Horowitz
May 15

The Bem experiments have failed—and proven replicable—dozens of times. Bottom line: his most significant trials proved confirmatory in a meta-analysis of 90 experiments (including the originals) in 33 different labs in 14 different nations, including in foreign languages such as Italian. Most of those trials, like the one you post, failed. But a substantial number cumulatively fell far below the P-value thus ruling out chance.

On a different tack, consider:

(a) no one experiment solves anything, especially in light of 90 previous reruns with an overall positive outcome;

(b) this supposedly super-rigorous new experiment had multiple errors of its own, as published here in an extensive correction (https://royalsocietypublishing.org/doi/10.1098/rsos.231080);

(c) the raw datafile lists all of the contributed trials, and the first column in that spreadsheet is supposed to contain a timestamp;

it doesn't, meaning another aspect of the transparent study contains an error.

The purpose of this study was to develop a more rigorous methodology to study psi and other claimed phenomena. The irony is that the methodology, developed by multiple experts, still had problems of its own. So, again, no single experiment solves anything. What goes in the right direction, however, are multiple truly independent replications, because unless everyone is making exactly the same mistake, one hopes that all those replications will average out methodological problems. This isn't necessarily the optimal solution—I have my own criticisms of P-values—but it's the best approach that's been developed so far.

CHAPTER SEVEN

Your Plus-Self

If you are like me, you often walk around feeling as though there are "two of you"—dual selves fighting for dominance.

And you are right: there are, in a sense, two personas struggling within us, like Jacob and Esau, Apollo and Artemis, Romulus and Remis, Horus and Set, and other dualistic twins hallowed in religion and myth.

Alchemical tradition posits the "divine hermaphrodite" as the joining of eternal, complementary polarities: spirit and matter, deity and mortal, male and female.

I deem these models "real" in terms of the psyche—and something more.

We often experience the sensation of being "two selves" during periods of self-assessment, including when we feel divided between mediocrity and excellence.

People often harbor the conviction that they *could* become a writer, or *could* get straight A's, or *could* excel at work, or *could* find a positive relationship—but *who exactly* could? We sometimes feel that such things are possible if only we could throw ourselves upon the energies of our higher, better, more formidable self or double, waiting to be integrated or released.

This possibility is real, but it is rarely, or only fleetingly, exercised.

Two of Us

Many modern fiction writers and psychologists, not to mention their ancient and folkloric forebears, have posited the existence of this "other self."

Psychologist Carl Jung famously called it the shadow, which he identified as a fount of unacknowledged desires and proclivities; if recognized and integrated into your day-to-day consciousness, these shadow traits could lead to the growth of untapped powers, confidence, and abilities.

For fantasy writer Robert Louis Stevenson, the other self was the malevolent Mr. Hyde, a feral counterpart to the refined and gentile Dr. Jekyll. For Edgar Allan Poe, the other side was represented by "William Wilson," the title of Poe's 1839 short story in which his protagonist, the debauched Wilson, grows up alongside an uncanny double who shares his name, appearance, and birthdate, and who eventually turns out to be the maleficent hero's alienated conscience.

Many fiction writers, like Stephen King in his 1989 novel, *The Dark Half*, see the other self as a figure of repressed violence and evil. But that reflects only one sliver of the split-self riddle of human nature. More important for our purposes, your counter-self can be a figure of relative fearlessness, effectiveness, and ability.

Napoleon Hill highlighted these possibilities in *Think and Grow Rich*:

O. Henry discovered the genius which slept within his brain, after he had met with great misfortune, and was confined to a prison cell in Columbus, Ohio. Being FORCED, through misfortune, to become acquainted with his "other self," and to use his IMAGINATION, he discovered himself to be a great author instead of a miserable criminal and outcast. Strange and varied are the ways of life, and stranger still are the ways of Infinite Intelligence, through which men are sometimes forced to undergo all sorts of punishments before discovering their own brains, and their own capacity to create useful ideas through imagination.

The Magic Story

One of the oddest modern inspirational works ever written, *The Magic Story*, features this theme of a positive double, which author Frederick van Rensselaer Dey (1861–1922) calls your "plus-entity."

In Dey's brief and strangely compelling instructional tale from 1900, he depicts the life of a down-and-out seventeenth-century craftsman who discovers that a haunting Presence, or other self, is hovering around his periphery. Dey's hero finds that his counter-self is a real part of him, one that is "calm, steadfast, and self-reliant." As soon as he comes to identify, literally, with his plus-entity, his life is happily transformed.

"Make a daily and nightly companion of your plus-entity," the hero counsels.

As it happens, the author Dey's life was less than happy: After a middling and prolific career writing pulp crime fiction, including the popular Nick Carter detective tales, the wearied writer shot himself to death in 1922.

He left behind a stoic suicide note, asking only that his older brother be taken care of. Dey's widow, Haryot Holt Dey, was herself a notable writer and suffragist who lived until 1950. To use the terms of Dey's own allegory, the author succumbed to his "minus-entity."

Meeting Your Plus-Self

How can you get in touch with your stronger plus-entity? Here are some (deceptively) simple techniques.

DRESS THE PART

Never neglect the power of simple things. The manner in which you dress and comport yourself has tremendous impact on your psyche. Most people instinctively sense this without fully acting on it. Become a thespian, trying out, perhaps subtly at first, different styles of dress, makeup, accessories, and body art. In one of my favorite episodes of *The Simpsons*, a teacher tells young Lisa, "Being tough comes from the inside. First step—change your outside." Like all good jokes, this one conceals a core truth. Magickian Anton LaVey referenced this process as claiming your "total environment."

FEED YOUR OTHER SELF

Furthering the theme of total environment, permit yourself to grow immersed in music, movies, and media that feed your sense of power and self-agency. As an example, consider the elegant but deadly robot named David in the 2012 science-fiction movie *Prometheus*; take note of how David studiously models his persona after the cinematic Lawrence of Arabia. Although brief, these scenes are no passing trifle; they are mini-models of the kinds of self-making that we all engage in, sometimes without awareness.

TALK LIKE IT

Consider the manner in which you speak. I once knew a crime reporter at a newspaper in upstate New York who had a slight build and appearance—but he spoke in a commanding, self-confident bass voice. It earned him the respect of the police and his newsroom colleagues. Whether natural or affected (I could never tell), his voice altered his entire persona.

FIND A MANIFESTO

You may question the value of reading *The Magic Story* given its author's tragic end. Do not be deterred. Read it tonight. (You can find it online.) Make its lessons your own. Dey possessed a keen instinct for human nature, including its shadowy and occultic paths to power. If this work does not speak to you (although I suspect it will), select another. For some, chapter four, "The Power of a Single Wish," may fill that role.

STAND FOR SOMETHING

The chief cause of mediocrity is purposelessness. We are never more aroused, sensitive, and capable than when we are striving for something. What are you striving for? A watch-the-clock job and entertainment will not summon more than your most average traits. Above all, you must find a chief aim in life, a theme that populates Hill's work. You should never be embarrassed by your aim. Your aim can be public or intimate. It requires no one's approval—it must be uniquely your own. The only tragedy is not having one.

* * *

Since earliest childhood, you have probably felt, as I have, that you are two selves. Select the self that builds you. It represents a more powerful choice than may at first appear.

CHAPTER EIGHT

The Metaphysics of "Making It"

Every worthy life is a philosophy in itself. In that vein, this chapter explores an outlook on success and mind-power devised by a contemporary of Napoleon Hill—and a figure like no other to emerge from America's metaphysical scene in the twentieth-century, Claude M. Bristol (1891–1951).

The Oregonian wrote neither as spiritual visionary nor scientist. He communicated only as a journalist and businessman who understood the needs of everyday people—for whom he crafted a metaphysics of achievement that won fans among the public and celebrities alike.

This occurred as Bristol suffered private struggles from which no positive-mind icon is exempt. I consider the author-businessman, like Napoleon Hill, a mosaic of American metaphysics: a self-taught, energetically experimental figure haunted by restrictions that confront every positive-mind practitioner.

Bristol attained mass readership through his sole fully realized book: 1948's *The Magic of Believing*, which has never fallen from print. This handbook to the reality-bending won admirers from Liberace to Phyllis Diller to Arnold Schwarzenegger. As a writer and seeker on the contemporary metaphysical scene, I encounter a surprising range of readers who swear by its insights.

The Magic of Believing is at once memoir and manual. Hence, it must be understood in connection with the author himself.

This chapter explores *why* Bristol's methods warrant serious attention, including as popular applications of Transcendentalism and early insights from parapsychology and scientific study of a sixth sense. It also considers *how* Bristol's life exemplified such ideas—and their personal limits.

From Portland to War

Bristol was born in Portland, Oregon, on March 8, 1891. (A matter as simple as his birthdate is complicated by records reporting 1890 and 1892. I rely on Bristol's World War I draft records.) He spent most of his career as a journalist, businessman, and lawyer. The author was widely known throughout the West as a crack newspaper and magazine writer. He first learned his craft as a police reporter in Portland. Few forms of training do more to sharpen and prepare you for work as a writer, journalist, or researcher than police reporting.

I also got my start as a police reporter at a strike-torn daily newspaper in a rustbelt town in Northeastern Pennsylvania; I relate to Bristol's path. In such settings, you perform under tight deadlines in stressful and unfriendly conditions. You learn to gather facts quickly and produce resolutely clear copy. Or you sink. That's where Bristol's writerly skills came from.

Bristol won sufficient note as a journalist so that Palmer Hoyt (1897–1979), the widely respected editor-in-chief of *The Denver Post*, introduced the first edition of *The Magic of Believing*, an unusual foray for a newspaper man into metaphysics. In what might be considered slightly backhanded praise, Hoyt opened: "Generally speaking, people are more interested in themselves and their success than anything else. For this reason Claude M. Bristol's book, *The Magic of Believing*, ought to enjoy widest readership."

While still young, Bristol experienced a downturn in life which got him on the scent trail of practical metaphysics. In early 1918, following conscription, he was deployed to France during World War I. It was the final year of that catastrophic conflict. At twenty-seven, Bristol was older than most infantrymen. Following his civilian work, Bristol went on to write for the Army newspaper *Stars and Stripes*. But early in his mobilization he was a standard grunt hauling around ammunition and supplies in dangerous battlefield conditions.

Due to a glitch in his assignment papers, Bristol was receiving no pay. For weeks he could not purchase a stick of gum, cigarette, or candy bar. He felt acute longing whenever he saw another soldier strike a match or toss away a gum wrapper. The Army supplied his meals. He had a place to sleep on the ground. But for a long stretch he was penniless. Bristol vowed to never again face that humiliation; when he returned home, he swore, he would always live in prosperity.

Money Passion

This experience ignited in Bristol the one factor I consider crucial to every program of self-development whether metaphysical, therapeutic, aspirational, or all three. You will recognize it from the work of Napoleon Hill. It is possessing a *passionate, definite, and unshakable aim*. Bristol wished for money, which he writes about plainly in *The Magic of Believing*. Critics could scoff but those familiar with affluence and on distant terms with lack rarely understand the aspirations of working and middle-class people, not as idealized but as on-the-ground realities. The term aspiration itself is rooted in the Latin *aspirare*, meaning to breathe. This is the burning urgency that drove Bristol.

"There is a relationship between pain and excellence," my partner filmmaker Jacqueline Castel says. This juxtaposition reverberates through Bristol's story. He suffered want. It propelled him toward desire. That desire, in turn, ignited his personal metaphysics. When Bristol arrived home, he found various positions in journalism, finance, and eventually law. He came to divide his career across each.

Whatever he was doing, Bristol wrote, he would sit at his desk and on a pad or scrap paper, whatever was at hand, he would doodle dollar signs, all day long. He did this while on the telephone, in meetings, or contemplating ideas. He was obsessed with his wish for money. Some might consider it gauche or unseemly, but his desires mushroomed into a career that proved not only multifaceted but highly remunerative. This included a successful writing career.

To call Bristol unsentimental in matters of money is an understatement. In his first book from 1932, *T.N.T.: It Rocks the Earth*, he echoed prejudices of his era but captured what he considered universal truths, which I quote in context:

> Skilled prosecutors, clever defenders appeal to the emotions of jurors, never to the conscious reason. And how do they do it? Simply by a process of repeating and emphasizing time after time the points they wish to stress. They do it with usage of words and variations of argument. Behind all there is that tap, tap, tap,

tap—tapping—the subconscious—making the jurors believe.

If you will keep this idea of repetition in mind you will understand why members of a certain race of people are so successful in business. When families are gathered together, the subject of conversation is business, business. They talk their problems over—they keep before them constantly the idea of making money and making progress and never for a moment are they permitted to forget. And they stick together.

The idea there was born of necessity, just like a machine or an article is born of necessity. We are all familiar with the old adage, "Necessity is the mother of invention"—and it is true of all human impulses and endeavors. A drowning man grabs at a straw. A starving man at a crust of bread. The impulses come when you get up against it. You who have been there know what you had to rely on in times of acute pressure, and whether or not you heard a little voice from within.

It is difficult not to blanch at Bristol's anachronisms—but he understood the power of necessity. On a different tack, Bristol also grasped the role of dress and appearance in matters of success and influence—and the urgency to create a certain drama around oneself:

Gandhi uses this POWER, I am sure, and I think he is the greatest headliner of present times. You can find many pictures showing him in the modern civilized garb of man, but today, and for several years he has kept his hair cropped short, worn a loin cloth and a pair of huge spectacles. I have no right to say that Gandhi affected this attire for any particular purpose, but I believe he has done it to focus the world's attention upon himself for India's cause.

I make no attempt to explain why those who use this POWER are showmen. You'll have to determine that for yourself.

I do not mean to leave the impression that Bristol was a one-dimensional schemer. "Having served as a soldier in World War I, mostly in France and Germany," he wrote in *The Magic of Believing*, "and having been an active official for many years in ex-service men's organizations as well as a member of a state commission to aid in the rehabilitation of ex-service men and women, I realized that it would be no easy task for many individuals to make outstanding places for themselves in a practical world from which they had long been separated."

When Bristol arrived home from war, he found a nation in transition. Business was booming and the mass of young veterans, many of whom came from agrarian backgrounds and had never worked in manufacturing or large offices, were unsure how to enter the new economy. For his part, Bristol believed that the threshold of prosperity begins in the mind, an idea he determined to spread, first through lectures and later his writing.

Metaphysics of Power and Wealth

Bristol wrote only two books. The first, just quoted, appeared in a self-published, pamphlet-sized format. *T.N.T.: It Rocks the Earth* entertainingly summarized his mind-power philosophy: that what you believe, feel, think, and visualize takes shape in your surroundings.

Bristol's title phrase T.N.T. references the explosive effect of continual thought and concentration on a certain point. This "tap-tap-tap" process, he wrote, is aided by:
1. writing aims on notecards you both carry and post where they catch your eye;
2. reciting aims to yourself in a mirror;
3. maintaining silence around your intentions to deter defeatist opinions of others;
4. and dwelling affirmatively and unerringly on your wishes.

Snobs could laugh (and still do) but Bristol's program differed only in explicitness from Ralph Waldo Emerson's (1803–1882) essays *Power* and *Wealth*, which the Transcendentalist philosopher published as part of *The Conduct of Life* in 1860. These proto self-help ideas (Emerson coined the term self-help in his 1841 lecture, "Man the Reformer") bear unpacking.

In *Power*, Emerson names four essential elements to exercising personal influence. The first—and that which sustains all the others—is to be "in sympathy with the course of things." Emerson believed that an individual could read the nature of things and seek to merge with it, like a twig carried downstream. "The mind that is parallel with the laws of nature," he writes, "will be in the current of events, and strong with their strength."

The second element of power is *health* (a challenge for Bristol, as soon seen). Emerson means this on different levels. He is speaking broadly of the vitality of body and spirit; the state of physicality and personal morale that sustains risks, seeks adventure, and completes plans. But he also speaks of routine bodily health, without which the individual's energies are sapped.

The third element is *concentration*, which is Bristol's keynote. One of nature's laws is that concentration of energies brings impact. The concentration of a striking blow delivers the greatest force. Too often we deplete our energies by dispersing or spreading thin our aims and efforts. We also do this by idle talk, which Bristol warned against. In *Power*, an imaginary oracle says: "Enlarge not thy destiny, endeavor not to do more than is given thee in charge." Like photons condensed into a laser, concentration brings greatest power.

Emerson's fourth and final element of power is *drilling*. By this he means repeating a practice over and over until you perform it with innate excellence. The martial artist repeats his movements and routines to the point where they enter physical memory and are available under all conditions. Likewise, we must drill—meaning practice or rehearse—to the point where we have mastered our chosen task.

In *Wealth*, Emerson declares, in a manner Bristol embraced, that the individual is "born to be rich." By riches, the philosopher is not employing a coy metaphor. He means cold, hard cash. But he also identifies accumulation of capital as befitting only that person who uses it to productive ends. Emerson writes,

> Every man is a consumer, and ought to be a producer. He fails to make his place good in the world, unless he not only pays his debt, but also adds something to the common wealth. Nor can he do justice to his genius, without making some larger demand on the world than a bare subsistence. He is by constitution expensive, and needs to be rich.

Only those purchases that expand your abilities leave you any richer. Indeed, wealth that fails to accompany expansion is wealth squandered. "Nor is the man enriched," Emerson writes, "in repeating the old experiments of animal sensation." Rather, you are enriched when you increase your capacity to earn, do, and grow.

So, how, finally, do you earn wealth? Emerson outlines roughly three steps: 1) First filling some nonnegotiable, subsistence-level need in your own life: this is what drove the primeval farmers, hunter-gathers, and villagers. 2) Next, applying one's particular talents to nature, and expansively filling the needs of others. If you do not know or understand your talents, you must start there before anything is possible. And, lastly, 3) using your wealth for the purposes of productiveness: paying down debts, making compound investments, and procuring the tools and talents of your trade.

All of this underscores *T.N.T.*, a drugstore bookrack resounding of Transcendentalism.

* * *

Bristol's 1932 booklet proved sufficiently successful, as did the author as lecturer and financier, so that he was able to retire from his Portland investment banking firm by age forty-one in 1933. Bristol describes using methods from his book to save the firm from bankruptcy during the Great Depression.

As a writer, "He has met with more than ordinary success," reported *The Sunday Oregonian* on January 1, 1933. "Because of demands made upon him he has decided to devote himself to this work in the future."

It was not until 1948, however, that Bristol published *The Magic of Believing*, which expanded on his early themes and added insights, soon to be seen, from parapsychology and ESP research. It may interest Napoleon Hill readers to know that *The Magic of Believing* briefly appeared under the knockoff title *Believe and Get Rich* (a thankfully errant edition). Under its enduring name, *The Magic of Believing* proved a bounding success. But the book belied suffering in the author's private life.

Lonely End

When Bristol published his signature work, he was fifty-seven years old. But the author's time in the book-selling spotlight was relatively short. He died of kidney failure at age sixty on December 14, 1951.* Following a late-life divorce, Bristol left most of his estate to the Shriner's Hospital for Crippled Children in Portland.** The author was a 32nd-degree Mason and Shriner. (Reacting to one of my early articles on Bristol, a pseudo-skeptic accused me of "survivor bias." He had not read the piece.)

The end could only have been profoundly difficult. After nearly twenty years of marriage, Bristol's wife, Edith, a publishing executive, divorced him the prior year.*** The childless couple experienced painful and public separation. In "Claude Bristol,

---

* "Bristol Services," *Oregon Daily Journal*, December 18, 1951. This article misstates Bristol's age at death as sixty-one. It was sixty.

** "Author Leaves Hospital Fund," *Oregon Daily Journal*, December 19, 1951

*** "Long Illness Takes Author," *Portland Oregonian*, December 16, 1951. This article, in Bristol's hometown no less, misstates his birth year as 1890. It is March 8, 1891, according to World War I draft records, corroborated by additional census and federal records (which do not always agree among themselves). Bristol compounded this confusion by filling out a World War II draft registration with the birth year of 1892. Assuming a birthdate of March 8, 1891, he died on at age sixty on December 14, 1951 (and not, as is sometimes misreported, age sixty-one). This article is also my source for Bristol's alternate title, *Believe and Get Rich*.

'Magic' Author, Sued by Spouse," the *Oregon Daily Journal* embarrassingly divulged on September 22, 1950, that Edith "charged the prominent Portland author with cruel and inhumane treatment, claiming he used abusive language, was jealous of her and her friends and has an overbearing disposition."

A December 16 obituary by the Associated Press noted only that Bristol died in a Portland hospital "after a long illness," remarking dryly, "'Magic of Believing' is a non-fiction book that says generally that a person can change the events of his everyday life by holding what Mr. Bristol termed the proper thoughts."

Down with Timelines

I spent a large part of my career in spiritual publishing. At one point it struck me that a majority of the successful books I issued—works that not only succeeded upon launch but attained some degree of posterity—were written by people in middle age or beyond. Bristol fit that pattern.

Personally, I did not publish my first book, *Occult America*, until age forty-three. I am proud of that fact. I encourage aspiring writers to feel at liberty from conventional timelines, as explored in chapter eleven. We experience physical limits, as Bristol markedly did. We experience limits in geography, income, and social background. But I remind readers that the man who produced one of the most enduring and widely read works of practical metaphysics of the twentieth century did not publish it until age fifty-seven and in declining health. Another popular metaphysician, New Thought minister Joseph Murphy, did not publish his landmark *Power of Your Subconscious Mind* until age sixty-five in 1963.

What I describe is part of why *The Magic of Believing* won readers' trust: it bore perspective from the road of life. Such experience is also marked by pain and failure, as Bristol's was. We must view inspirational writers and speakers as three-dimensional beings, not stick figures. Neither life's joys nor tragedies are exclusive of the other, including in the careers of New Age icons, who I wish were more disclosing about such matters. I once interviewed Deepak Chopra whose fifteen-minute answers could have tried the patience of a Zen monk. At no point did the bestselling author utter a word of personal vulnerability. That is unrealistic.

Whatever the ultimate nature of reality, I often note, none of us experience life from the mechanics of one mental super law—we dwell under a complexity of laws and forces, some of which can prove overwhelmingly countervailing.

But I likewise believe that any author must be remembered for his or her finest work. *The Magic of Believing* was Bristol's. I believe his metaphysics have a place in the lives of striving people. They do in mine.

Practical Magic

I noted that Bristol had good writerly training.* Many people say they want to write and wonder how to start. (Wanting to get published is different from wanting to write—never confuse them.) I always say to begin, like Bristol, with the basics of journalism. Learn how to write a lead paragraph. Learn the five W's: who,

---

* Not so good that the former newspaper man didn't sometimes mishandle facts. In a humorous barb, the *Oregon Daily Journal* reported on May 1, 1944, that when Bristol became campaign manager to Republican Joe Dunne in his Portland mayoral race: "In his announcement Bristol reviewed his accomplishments in the newspaper field, as an author, a member of the American Legion and a business executive, touched upon the legislative and public record of former [State] Senator Dunne but overlooked telling where the campaign headquarters are to be established." Dunne lost the Republican primary to incumbent Earl Riley.

what, when, where, and why. Learn the basics of old-time wire-service writing. Do this and you will have a foundation that rarely fails you. This was Bristol's approach in all things, from daily journalism to practical metaphysics.

Whatever the pain of his personal life, Bristol's *Magic of Believing*, issued by Prentice-Hall in May 1948, proved an immediate success. It ran through four printings in its first year of publication and entered thirteen more printings over the next three years. By the author's death in 1951, an impressive 150,000 copies were in print—with many times that number appearing in multiple editions today. (Due to a copyright-renewal snafu, the book entered public domain in 1976.)

Some celebrities of Bristol's era vowed that his book launched them on their path. Comedian Phyllis Diller (1917–2012) was a vocal fan of *The Magic of Believing*. The brashly funny performer said she suffered from crushing shyness until she discovered Bristol's guide. She recommended it throughout her life and often praised it in interviews.

Pianist Liberace (1919–1987) was a particular admirer of *The Magic of Believing*. In his memoir, the performer recalled initially exposing his friend Diller to the book.* Liberace's biographer, Darden Asbury Pyron, said the entertainer considered it a "semi-sacred text," further noting: "he seems to have discovered the book at a critical juncture—the mid-fifties—when he was losing his grip on his career and even on his life."**

What Liberace found sufficiently impressed him so that in 1955 there appeared a "Special Liberace Edition" of *The Magic of Believing*, which featured his short introduction, image on the

---

* *Liberace: An Autobiography* (Putnam, 1973)

** *Liberace: An American Boy* (The University of Chicago Press, 2000)

cover, and "17 photos of the maestro and his family." The following year, the louche performer recorded a song in tribute called "The Magic of Believing," apparently in promotional agreement with Bristol's publisher.

"My attitude," Liberace said of his career, "is that nothing is impossible, it just takes a little longer."

In 2010, blogger Mike Cane ventured an intriguing observation:

> Now this has to make you wonder, especially if you grew up in the early 1960s and were exposed to Liberace and Phyllis Diller in their TV heyday. I don't think there were two more 'out there' performers at the time than them. Liberace was flamboyantly effeminate during a time of widespread fear of homosexuality. Phyllis Diller never had a face for TV and had a voice that could scratch records. Yet both of them got where they both wanted to be, and they credited Bristol's book for that.*

Both of Bristol's books sat in Marilyn Monroe's library. Arnold Schwarzenegger has praised *The Magic of Believing*. George Noory, the host of Coast to Coast AM, credits the book with setting his career in motion. I have personally received dozens of emails from readers ranging from artists to salesmen who call *The Magic of Believing* a turning point in their lives.

Twenty-five years after Bristol's death, the Rev. Norman Vincent Peale, America's fitful dean of mainstream positivity, writing in his 1976 *The Positive Principle Today* deemed *The Magic of Believ-*

---

* "Mike Cane's xBlog," December 17, 2010.

ing "one of the few greatest inspirational and motivational books ever written in the United States."

Real Miracles?

I want to offer a true story around the book that personally reached me. I provide this anecdote with no implication that something similar is going to happen to the book's readers but rather with the promise that every word I relate is true as I experienced it.

One evening several years prior to this writing, I went on social media and posted a picture of my 1948 vintage edition of *The Magic of Believing* (it is signed by Bristol). Along with the image, I issued a challenge: "Let's try to approach this book with what in Zen Buddhism is called 'beginner's mind'."

I continued: "Let's imagine that it's 1948 and *The Magic of Believing* has just rolled off the presses. We are all holding first editions in our hands. Let's stay up into the night together and read this book."

I believe that pooling of inner resources naturally arises from group activities, such as marathon running. On the intellectual-emotive scale, unified group effort tends to heighten morale and focus. So, I issued this challenge and wrote, "Sit in a chair with me up late into the night and let's approach these ideas as though for the very first time."

When I posted this challenge, it caught the eye of a friend in New England. He was recovering from a severe and longstanding illness. While recuperating, my friend had fallen into desperate financial straits. He had been unable to work and was down to $102 in the bank. He had no health insurance, source of income, or near-term prospects.

He told himself, "I have nothing to lose. I may as well take up this challenge." My friend owned an audio edition of *The Magic of Believing*, which I had narrated. He played the recording over and over. He sometimes listened for hours at a stretch. It became his constant companion for about a week. Within a few days he received a call from a former boss. As they were catching up, his ex-boss said, "By the way, you really ought check your old 401(k)." My friend had maintained such an account but not rolled it over when he left his job.

He sighed and replied, "Oh that—what's the big deal?" He thought there was just a few dollars in it. His ex-boss told him, "No, really, I'm being serious. You've got to check your 401(k)."

The former employer said that more than $50,000 sat dormant in the account. My friend had no idea he had accumulated so much money. He was recovering from a debilitating illness, so his eye was not on finances as it would have been at other times in life. As in Bristol's experience, we see the interplay of forwarding and retrograde factors.

This call arrived several days into his marathon listen of *The Magic of Believing*. Was it coincidence? Possibly. Was he wishfully projecting a pattern onto something? Perhaps. Was it a miracle? Well, the news reached him in a fashion that emotionally felt miraculous.

Again, I am not suggesting that *The Magic of Believing* is going to produce some marvel in your life. But let me offer a possibility—and it is something that Bristol certainly believed himself. I take seriously that there exist extra-physical dimensions to thought. We possess too much evidence to dismiss that prospect. In fact, we have so much replicated evidence of some extra-physical, non-local capacity to the mind—much of it derived from laboratory experiments across fields including medicine, physics, and academic psychical research—that strict physicalism fails to cover the bases of life. Add insights from quantum mechanics, theory, and computing, and the notion that matter alone creates itself, and that your mind is just a byproduct of neuro-physicality, seems today like clinging to geocentrism or phrenology.

Academic psychical researchers venture that when your psyche is profoundly and deeply focused—recall the Latin *aspirare*—you may be directing some kind of communication to others capable of helping or meeting you halfway. Bristol goes further. He reasons that your mind possesses vibrational or frequency-like signals that can result not only in telepathy but in psychokinesis or mind-over-matter.

In some respects, I consider Bristol's language metaphorical since imagery is always at play when attempting to understand or conceptually apply something that we as a human community have not fully grasped. But I must also add that Bristol's supposition is not as far out as it may seem.

As already noted, twentieth-century parapsychologist J.B. Rhine (1895–1980), whose research Bristol often cites, conducted ESP experiments for years at Duke University. Under rigorously controlled laboratory conditions Rhine and collaborators found key subjects capable of receiving and transmitting information in an anomalous manner unaffected by time, space, or mass, extending to the psychokinetic ability of affecting throws of dice.*

Twenty-first century psychical researchers at Princeton University found subjects who by concentration alone could introduce a pattern into chaotic numbers emitting from a random-number generator, which spews infinite combinations of

---

* I consider Rhine's record and replication of his work in Appendix B: "Wild Talents." Also see my 2022 *Daydream Believer*.

numerals or symbols (a device used to create online passwords). Through intention, subjects caused episodes of symmetry where none should appear. The researchers' ongoing Global Consciousness Project has documented that during periods of worldwide emotional intensity, such as the terrorist attacks of 9/11, random-number generators planted in select locations globally display inexplicable patterns or interruptions in randomness.*

Following a decade of study, Cornell University research psychologist Daryl J. Bem published a 2011 paper reporting the results of his series of experiments into precognition. As seen, Bem found that test subjects who memorized a word list scored higher in recall by repeating their study of the list following the test. Bem's data, like Rhine's, has since proved confirmatory in replicated experiments and meta-analysis.**

Although I am necessarily describing these experiments in shorthand, they have been subject to greater scrutiny than most trials to test the effectiveness of popular pharmaceuticals. I direct interested readers to a comprehensive analysis of psychical research and its replications that appeared in the flagship journal of the American Psychological Association: "The Experimental Evidence for Parapsychological Phenomena: A Review" by Etzel Cardeña, *American Psychologist* (2018, Vol. 73). I provide a user-friendly summary in "Parapsychology: Evidence & Resources for the 'Elusive Science'" at Medium.

---

* For a summary of the Global Consciousness Project, see: "Terrorist Disaster, September 11, 2001;" "Formal Results: Testing the GCP Hypothesis;" and "Global Consciousness Project Brief Overview" at noosphere.princeton.edu.

** "Feeling the Future: Experimental Evidence for Anomalous Retroactive Influences on Cognition and Affect" by Daryl J. Bem, *Journal of Personality and Social Psychology*, 2011, Vol. 100, No.3. For further consideration of Bem's work and its replication see my "Is Precognition Real?", Substack, April 25, 2025.

For these reasons, I honor Bristol's instinct that emotively charged and focused thought may be communicated, at least intermittently, in some extra-physical manner. Perhaps this occurred for my friend when his ex-boss reached out to him at the most desperate moment of his life to share news of an investment account with $50,000.

Skeptics insist that our brains are designed to impose patterns on things. That is true. But skeptics rarely apply this logic to themselves. Their immediate impulse is to rationalize anomalies according to diagnostic or logical categories they find familiar. But events like the one I just described are difficult to quantify.

This is due to the complexity of emotions involved. Seen from one perspective, a remarkable web of events exists at the back of virtually everything that happens to you, whether seemingly exceptional or mundane. But factors of emotional impact, timing, and profundity of need are highly individualized, making anomalous experiences difficult to quantify, reify, or measure. Not everything in life can be broken down on an actuarial table.

Recall Bristol's dollar doodling. I have often noted the importance of understanding what you truly want in life—of having a definite, absolute aim. I suggest that people write out their aim, not on a handheld device, tablet, or laptop; but in a tactile way with a pen or pencil and paper.

I believe that when you write down a wish, the very act of rendering it in a physical manner is a first step, however nascent, toward some means of actualization. Think of it: when you produce something on paper, you not only have a vow and contract, you not only have a clarified and committed purpose, but your act has, however infinitesimally, altered reality or your experience of it. The writing on that paper has created something not previously extant. This is the basis of sigil-making in chaos magic, which, like chaos theory, holds that observed events pivot on seemingly tiny or unseen complexities. Always regard first steps, however small, seriously.

Bristol spent his workdays constantly reinforcing what he wanted. Simple enough. But we are not always capable of sincerely acknowledging what we want. When you consider your aim be sure that you are inwardly honest and not curbed by some sense of embarrassment, shame, or internalized peer pressure. A true wish should always feel a little embarrassing.

Most of us strive to look good in the eyes of others. We want appreciation and admiration. Yet we just as often harbor handed-down or customary ideas of how to achieve that. In many cases, these ideas are no more than decisions made by someone else, often in the distant past.

One of the mental traps that limits creativity and sense of self is the habit of rote thought, even in our most private ponderings. The things we tell ourselves over the course of life—I want to be of service; I want a relationship; I want to be a leader in my field—become so familiar that we eventually fail to question or verify them. Are our resolutions sincere—or habitual?

Never obfuscate what you want. That does not mean a desire is always wise or actionable. But it must at least be acknowledged. Truth liberates.

Bristol, in his way, made large questions about the psyche appear simple—because he believed that meaningful personal experiments are possible. Such experiments demonstrate, or at least suggest, the efficacy of mind-metaphysics in daily life, including in matters of career, creativity, money, and relationships.

Meta-Classic

Bristol's simplicity proved infectious. In addition to the accolades I have mentioned, *The Magic of Believing* became such a post-war favorite that in 1957 Prentice-Hall issued an illustrated *Magic of Believing for Young People*.

The young readers' edition failed to catch on. At more than 200 pages, it was almost the length of the original and no simpler. But it is the kind of publishing effort I admire. Despite the enduring popularity of New Thought or mind-power literature, few books are geared toward adolescents who might benefit from the types of self-query and experimentation that the best of such works encourage. In 1954, the publisher also issued a posthumously expanded version of *T.N.T*, which proved more lasting.

Although Bristol's language is sometimes dated and his tone credulous, *The Magic of Believing* remains a surprising and radical journey into the possibilities of determined thought. We are still at the early stages of grappling with some of his topics, gaining a glimpse of anomalous mental capacities in a new generation of experiments in the placebo response, neuroplasticity, precognition, and perceptual theory.

Hence, as I did that day on social media, I suggest approaching *The Magic of Believing* in a spirit of enthusiasm and personal adventure. It is a longstanding favorite that provides unembarrassed invitation to intimately probe questions of mental-emotive causality. The book may ignite in you, as it has in me, a sense of renewed possibility.

Are we too cynical today to try?

CHAPTER NINE

The Gospel of Carnegie

Napoleon Hill credits steel magnate Andrew Carnegie (1835–1919) with inspiring and informing his success philosophy. But what did the industrialist, in his own words and concepts, believe about accumulating wealth? His ideas differ from Hill's—but contain a similar nugget of metaphysics

Hill describes his first encounter with Carnegie—"the richest man that the richest nation on earth ever produced"—in terms that bring to mind Moses receiving the tablets on Mount Sinai. Hill said that he interviewed the industrialist in 1908 and received marching orders to codify a philosophy of success, which formed the basis for his 1928 book *The Law of Success* and the wealth-building classic that followed nine years later, *Think and Grow Rich*.

Whatever impression Hill left on Carnegie, the industrialist made no mention of the younger man in his writings. Nor did Hill begin making references to the fateful meeting until nearly a decade after Carnegie's death in 1919.

Critics question whether the encounter ever took place. I am agnostic on the point. Hill was working that year for *Bob Taylor's*

Magazine, an inspirational and general-interest monthly published by the former governor of Tennessee who continued the magazine as a U.S. senator.

The journal featured up-by-the-bootstraps stories of millionaires—a staple of the day's popular literature—and the job (and Taylor's position) could have facilitated contact between journalist and subject. In December 1908, under his birthname "Oliver Napoleon Hill" (one of the last times he would use that byline), Hill wrote a regional essay on "Mobile and Southern Alabama" accompanied by an author photo of the bow-tied young writer. No interview with Carnegie ever appeared, nor have I located any further byline for Hill in the magazine.

In any case, Carnegie's memoirs do paint the image of a man who enjoyed discussing the metaphysics of success. In his autobiography, published posthumously in 1920, Carnegie recalled that as an adolescent he "became deeply interested in the mysterious doctrines of Swedenborg." A Spiritualist aunt encouraged the young Carnegie to develop his psychical talents, or "ability to expound 'spiritual sense'."

Carnegie was eager to be taken seriously as an author and he reveled in probing whether there exist natural laws of money and accumulation. In June 1889, Carnegie published his essay "Wealth" for the *North American Review*, which might have been forgotten if not for its near-immediate republication by England's evening newspaper *The Pall Mall Gazette* under the more alluring title by which it became internationally famous: "The Gospel of Wealth." (Recall what I wrote earlier about titles.)

Taking a leaf from the neo-Darwinian views of philosopher Herbert Spencer, Carnegie described a "law of competition," which he believed brought a rough, necessary order to the world:

> While the law may be sometimes hard to the individual, it is best for the race, because it ensures the survival of the fittest in every department. We accept and welcome, therefore, as conditions to which we must accommodate ourselves, great inequality of environment, the concentration of business, industrial and commercial, in the hands of a few, and the law of competition between these, as being not only beneficial but essential for the future progress of the race.

Although contemporaneous success authors such as Ralph Waldo Trine (1866–1958) and Wallace D. Wattles (1860–1911) extolled creativity above competition, Carnegie welcomed "laws of accumulation" as a necessary means of separating life's winners from losers. At his steel mills, the magnate sometimes backed his belief through ruthless and, by way of surrogates and business partners, brutal labor practices. Seven of his workers were killed by Pinkerton guards during the Homestead Strike of 1892.

Yet Carnegie's essay had a surprising wrinkle. He emphasized that great wealth—which he attributed chiefly to raw materials, real estate, utilities, and inventions (the manufacturer disdained financial speculation)—was the product of the community. And should ultimately be returned to it.

Wealth, Carnegie argued, is amassed as a passive result of an industrialist or investor benefiting from mass shifts in demography, migration, and public needs. The world's reputedly richest man wrote that wealth should be restored to the community rather than passed down through family inheritance.

In a sentiment that would win him few admirers among radicals and reformers, Carnegie counseled that millionaires should electively dispense their money in acts of philanthropy during their lifetimes. He called that the legitimate culmination of success. In essence, Carnegie argued that monopolistic capitalism should be leavened by voluntary largesse or noblesse oblige.

But the millionaire's sense of volunteerism had limits. If the rich didn't find a way to disperse their fortunes through philanthropy, Carnegie called for a nearly 100 percent estate tax to settle the matter for them.

"The Gospel of Wealth" proved so popular that Carnegie issued two sequels in the *North American Review*—the first in December 1889 called "The Best Fields for Philanthropy" and the second seventeen years later in December 1906 called "The Gospel of Wealth II." Although Carnegie wrote a handful of related pieces in response to his critics, his earlier essays provide a more or less complete perspective on his views of how wealth is generated—and how it should be dispensed.

Whether one agrees with Carnegie on every point—and I do not—it is worth noting that he followed through on his statements with wide-ranging acts of structured philanthropy. In so doing, the industrialist helped presage the nonprofit field as it exists today.

His business advice is for each individual to assess, but of one point he leaves no doubt: great fortunes accrue due not primarily to the ability of their holders but to ancillary events and circumstances that emerge from public need and growth.

CHAPTER TEN

The World Is As You Are

Napoleon Hill frequently wrote about an "Infinite Intelligence" of which we are all channels. Hill's definition of Infinite Intelligence relates to Ralph Waldo Emerson's (1803–1882) concept of an "Over-Soul." Emerson wrote in his essay "History" in 1841: "There is one mind common to all individual men. Every man is an inlet to the same and to all of the same."

Such concepts relate to what eighteenth-century Swedish mystic-scientist Emanuel Swedenborg (1688–1772) called "Divine influx." Another historical comparison is the all-creative Infinite Mind or *Nous* within Hermeticism, the late-ancient Greek-Egyptian philosophy that preserved a fragment of Ancient Egypt's esoteric theology.

As Hill saw it, this over-mind—a nonlocal intellect from which we all extend—is tappable through your subconscious. The author prescribed visualizations, prayer, and affirmations—all standard methods in the New Thought catalogue—to place oneself within the insights and causative powers of Infinite Intelligence. The subconscious, Hill taught, translates thoughts, plans, and ideas to Infinite Intelligence for actualization, the power of which redounds to the individual via flashes of insight, leads, intuitions, and peak efforts. Infinite Intelligence, in Hill's view, uses the individual as its medium of creation.

"If you conceive a thing and believe it and make a definite picture of it in your own mind," Hill said in a 1952 lecture, "the law of Cosmic Habit Force takes over that picture and guides you to the physical equivalent of that thing, whatever it may be... And you'll be surprised at how many things will come to you that you wanted before, that you worked hard for and didn't get when you learn how to fasten upon your mind a definite outline of the things that represent to you success in this life." Hill's term, Cosmic Habit Force, admittedly a slightly overwrought phrase, is clarified shortly.

Hill's point of view dovetails with under-appreciated twentieth-century New Thought theorist Geneviève Behrend (1881–1960). The author and metaphysical seeker—herself a close student of New Thought icon Thomas Troward (1847–1916)—provided a clarifying portrait of her mind-power principles in her 1921 *Your Invisible Power*. They sound much like Hill's and warrant parallel exploration:

> We now fly through the air, not because anyone has been able to change the laws of Nature, but because the inventor of the flying machine learned how to apply Nature's laws and, by making orderly use of them, produced the desired result. So far as the natural forces are concerned, nothing has changed since the beginning. There were no airplanes in "the Year One," because those of that generation could not conceive the idea as a practical, working possibility. "It has not yet been done," was the argument, "and it cannot be done." Yet

the laws and materials for practical flying machines existed then as now.

Troward tells us that the great lesson he learned from the airplane and wireless telegraphy is the triumph of principle over precedent, the working out of an idea to its logical conclusion in spite of accumulated contrary testimony of all past experience.

Behrend's perspective, like Hill's, does not suggest that your visualizing powers will manifest properties from the ether. Rather, the powers of causative thought can bring about the extraordinary by working through *established channels* of production and creation. We do not bend natural laws, in Hill's view—rather, we discover multitudinous possibilities within them. Likewise, Behrend puts it this way, with her emphasis in the original: *"In visualizing, or making a mental picture, you are not endeavoring to change the laws of Nature. You are fulfilling them."*

Compare that to Hill's perspective from an unpublished audio program. This is a reasonable summary of what he terms Cosmic Habit Force:

> The same force which maintains the precise balance between all the actions and reactions of matter and the time and space relationships of the elements of Creation also builds man's thought habits with varying degrees of permanency. Negative thought habits of any kind attract to their Creator physical manifestations corresponding to their nature as perfectly and as inevitably as nature germinates the acorn and develops it into an oak tree. Through the operation of the very same law, positive thoughts reach out into the vast

ocean of potential power surrounding us and attract the physical counterparts of their nature.

You create patterns of thought by repeating certain ideas or behavior and the law of Cosmic Habit Force takes over those patterns and makes them more or less permanent unless or until you consciously rearrange them. The method employed by Cosmic Habit Force in converting a positive emotion or desire created in the mind of man into its physical equivalent is this: It intensifies that emotion or desire until it induces the state of mind known as faith, in which it is receptive to inflowing infinite intelligence whence are derived perfect plans to be followed by the individual for the attainment of his desired objective. Natural means are used to carry out such plans.

Often a person is awed by what appear to be coincidental combinations of favorable circumstances as he carries out his plans, but these strange and unexplained things happen in a perfectly natural way. Cosmic Habit Force has the capacity to impart a peculiar quality to one's thought habits which gives them the power to surmount all difficulties, remove all obstacles, overcome all resistances. Just what this power is, is a secret as profound as the secret which causes a seed of wheat to germinate, grow, and reproduce itself.

Hence, both systems agree that while the individual must function within the recognizable physical sphere—subject to its limits, conditions, and natural laws—he is also an extension of Infinite Intelligence and thus functions as a channel of creative potential whose medium is thought. To this I must add emotion and physicality, which condition thought and vice versa. These forces—intellect, emotion, and physicality—often operate along parallel and, not infrequently, conflictual lines. Yet instances of unity among them can prove uniquely powerful and advancing, as seen in chapter four, "The Power of a Single Wish."

A Thought Experiment

Whether you are new to these ideas or a veteran reader who needs a refresher let me propose an exercise. Reread the statements above from Behrend and Hill. When you are finished, select and dedicate one hour—just one hour—during which you assume that the writers' *every principle about thought and creation is correct*. Act as though you possess ultimate creative responsibility for your life with the boundaries described. Entertain no doubts. This is your private experiment. Tell no one what you are doing. Behrend provides wise counsel on how speech dissipates the impact of thought: "One tells one's troubles to weaken them, to get them off one's mind, and when a thought is given out, its power is dissipated."

If *one hour* leaves you satisfied, select another period in which to expand your experiment to two hours. Then expand two to four, four to eight, and, finally, eight to sixteen, which is, roughly, the length of a waking day. Once you reach the waking-day stage of your experiment, go to sleep visualizing a desired outcome. That final step amounts to a twenty-four-hour commitment. See what occurs. Will you try? It requires only an hour to start.

If you experience doubts or setbacks, do not worry. There is no need to start over. Life is filled with switchbacks. It is unrealistic and unnecessary to attempt to avoid them. You are not seeking an impossibly high standard of inner performance. You are simply exploring your dimensions as an ethical and creative being—and probing "your invisible power" as a self-devised being.

See It, Feel It

I want to take matters a step further and offer you an exercise in creative visualization. The type of visualization I use is prescribed by twentieth-century mystic Neville Goddard (1905–1972): playing in your mind a small scene that implies the fulfillment of your aim. It can be anything, provided it proves vivid, tactile, and emotionally persuasive. *Feel* yourself in any small drama or role, no matter how brief, that would naturally accompany or immediately follow fulfillment of your wish, such as someone shaking your hand and congratulating you. You are not watching the image as if it appears on a screen—rather you are feeling and imagining yourself *within* the scene.

The best times to enter this state, I have found, are when you are drifting to sleep at night—the period of natural relaxation called hypnagogia (as seen in chapter two)—or other times when you may feel a sense of deep relaxation bordering on sleep, such as following meditation. But do not be controlled by form. When you arrive at a moment where an inner scene and of sense quietude reach you: act on it.

Recent to this writing I was standing in my kitchen in Brooklyn, New York, and inwardly felt the type of scene that implied fulfillment of a wish. I was awake earlier than anyone else in my household (a common occurrence among seekers), so I entered a meditative state and internally acted out the scene. Were it any other time of day I would have done the same. Act when the mood strikes. Never mind whether circumstances or privacy are ideal. These are precious moments. Seize them.

Further pursuing the visualization method, I want to share an exercise that reached me in the form of an email from a reader. It was accompanied by a powerful and personal backstory which I withhold only for reasons of privacy:

> If you could do anything in your life from where you are, if money was no problem, what would you want to do? Your big goal, the thing that would fill you up. What job would you love to do if family, education, and money didn't come into it? Write down your goals this year with as much detail as you can imagine. Get quiet and visualize them like they are already real. Feel what it would be like if they had already happened. See yourself doing those things, being happy and living it. Your friends congratulating you and being amazed at what you've achieved. What are they saying to you? They're shocked and high fiving you!
>
> Do the imagining every night for about fifteen days before you go to sleep and really put feeling and emotions into the visions. Feel the excitement. This really works, it will put things into motion but you have to believe in it. Trust in this and give it a try.

I suggest writing out this quoted passage by hand, adding the words "I trust" at the bottom, dating it, and signing it. I did this. I never suggest anything that I do not do myself.

Try

One final note: To attain her goal of becoming a personal student of retired colonial judge Thomas Troward, Geneviève Behrend did not just think—she acted: with persistence, some degree of audacity, and aplomb. She kept after Troward—doggedly but intelligently—after the metaphysical writer first ignored and then refused her entreaties. She impressed her hoped-for teacher not only by her resiliency but by her *rigor of preparation*. Never neglect that.

This touches on how I came to collaborate with Josh Hyde, a gifted graphic artist, musician, and website designer. In spring 2020, Josh sought to work with me. He made a video pitching himself—a step I appreciated. He followed up by creating several pieces of promotional art for events I was doing. They were brilliant—original, edgy, and fresh. Within about five months (this writing marks about five years), I opted to formalize our relationship and today we collaborate on a wide range of projects. Josh began, he told me, by holding an ideal in his mind—but he also acted.

"A great idea is valueless," Behrend wrote, "unless accompanied by physical action."

CHAPTER ELEVEN

It Is Not Too Late

I want to say something about society's timelines. To hell with them.

I write these words on June 1, 2025, at age fifty-nine. I turn sixty in November. I did not publish my first book *Occult America* until age forty-three in 2009. I did not receive my first royalty check until the year of this writing.

I earn my living—that includes raising two sons with zero inherited wealth (dad was a Legal Aid Society attorney and mom was a medical secretary)—strictly as an artist, which in my case means writing, speaking, narrating, and doing television. I regard myself first and chiefly as a writer without which none of my other activities would be possible (or would be any good, for that matter).

Here are the facts: I worked in corporate publishing for twenty-seven years—until Penguin Random House fired me in 2017—and during that time I socked away a lot of money in index funds, which I heartily recommend if you want independent means and do not wish to rent, flip, or manage real estate. I like *Rich Dad Poor Dad*. But if you read between the lines, the author's sole recommendation is real estate, which is good if you are Mr. Fixit but I am not.

Now, barring extreme countervailing measures—which do exist—there is literally no timeline for producing whatever work is your passion, other than matters of physical survival and health. (No small consideration but daily, most of the time for most of us, okay.)

My secret formula, if I have any, is to work constantly, when I am not with my few loved ones, chiefly my partner, two sons, and my sister and her family. I have no friends, who generally turn out to be Marcus Brutus anyway. I am happy.

Casting aside recitative wisdom, my spiritual practices are aspirational and acquisitive to use terms least favorable to me, which every seeker ought to. I believe those efforts, which run throughout this book, heartily help. In fact, without the work of Napoleon Hill, I am unsure I would have found my way. (I explore further techniques in historical and methodological detail in *Practical Magick*.)

If you hold a day job that supports your passion, as publishing did my writing, that certainly helps; I realize, too, that it is not always possible. But as a friend pointed out, "You wouldn't believe how many great artists held day jobs."

In my day job I noticed this: the most lasting books I published (usually on spiritual traditions and social topics) were written by authors already well into middle-age. I saw this occur repeatedly. For this reason, among pettier ones, I revile "thirty under thirty" lists.

I believe that working on your dreams keeps you young, a fact suggested by Harvard psychologist Ellen Langer. In studies by Langer—the subject of controversy but their results never upended—elderly subjects experienced physical and mental improvements—including increased strength and flexibility, recovered memory and cognitive function, and improved mood and vitality—when immersed in nostalgic settings populated with stimuli from their youth, including vintage books, music, and movies. In Langer's work, settings that evoke feelings of youth actually seem to summon the reappearance of youthful traits, extending even to improved eyesight.*

I have made the same observation about aesthetics and appearance, which, as noted, magickian Anton LaVey termed "total environment." I am not preachy about appearance. You do what works for you, on every level, barring nothing.

Back to writing. In my thirties, I thought I had left it behind. After college (from which I carried little debt: $700 per semester at Stony Brook) I took a job as a police reporter at a Pennsylvania daily. I was too sensitive for it. I returned home and eventually settled into work in book publishing. It paid well (after a while) and I accomplished some things of which I am proud—but I could never escape the stomach-knotting truth that I settled for the second-best path of facilitator versus creator. That was my self-assessment, at least.

I have told the story elsewhere and will not repeat it here but when I reawakened to myself as a writer around 2003 (thanks to a propitious offer to a write a freelance article), it was as though the last glacial period had ended. From that point, I never stopped honing my ability as a historian and author. Within four years, I had a book contract. The one that just paid out a royalty this year.

---

* See "What If Age Is Nothing but a Mind-Set?" by Bruce Grierson in *The New York Times Magazine*, October 22, 2014. Researchers often dispute older studies, such as Langer's 1981 aging study, based on newer standards of methodology or those touted as such. But this phenomenon affects our view of all past clinical work, as it will affect how future researchers view today's practices, since methods inevitably change. More recently, researchers have linked reversal of greying hair to de-stressing: "Quantitative mapping of human hair greying and reversal in relation to life stress" by Ayelet M Rosenberg, et al., *eLife*, 10:e67437, 2021.

When I tell you it is not too late—and, in fact, it is not late at all—I speak from lived experience. I cannot imagine my life (or nearly anyone's) is exclusive.

In this book, I have proffered metaphysical arguments, mine and Napoleon Hill's to defend my point. But on the level of principle alone, I offer you this truth. Make it yours.

Epilogue

Napoleon Hill's "Secret"

Napoleon Hill references a "secret" that runs throughout *Think and Grow Rich*. This secret, he writes, appears at least once in every chapter. But he does not specifically name the secret. Hill writes that it is more beneficial and penetrating for you to arrive at the secret yourself. Some readers, he says, grasp it almost immediately. For others it takes multiple readings. Sometimes, right in the midst of a chapter, the secret may flash into your mind. It often comes, Hill writes, when you are ready for it.

I had such an experience in 2020. I found what I believe is the secret. In actuality, what I discovered is an expansion of something I have written about earlier but with a difference. I have previously written that the secret of *Think and Grow Rich* can be put this way: "Emotionalized thought directed toward one passionately held aim—aided by organized planning and the Master Mind—is the root of all accomplishment." I stand by that. But a more basic conception of Hill's secret reached me as I was writing on "applied faith." It is this:

> The "secret" of *Think and Grow Rich* is to place yourself within the overall scheme of creation, obeying

natural laws that inevitably and invariably beget growth, expansion, renewal, and generativity.

Each step in Hill's work is designed to bring you into *natural, cosmic alignment*. This is referenced earlier as Cosmic Habit Force. Once you are in alignment and work within its flow—toward continual growth and expansion—the laws of creation are at your back; these laws include the extra-physical principles explored in this book.

In this process, you become like the seedling that eventually bursts through the soil. All of nature, seen and unseen, operates to make this growth occur. Unlike the seedling, however, a sentient being must consciously and selectively labor. That is your role in creation. But when you are productively united, mentally, emotionally, and physically, in the direction of your aim, you naturally enlist these cosmic laws. These laws possess greater potential for a conscious being than they do for the seedling *because they not only aid your expansion but also allow for dramatic re-creation of self.*

I want to share what I consider the most important passage in *Think and Grow Rich*. It appears in the chapter on "Imagination" and directly pertains to what I am referencing:

> You are now engaged in the task of trying to profit by Nature's method. You are (sincerely and earnestly, we hope), trying to adapt yourself to Nature's laws, by endeavoring to convert DESIRE into its physical or monetary equivalent. YOU CAN DO IT! IT HAS BEEN DONE BEFORE!
>
> You can build a fortune through the aid of laws which are immutable. But, first, you must become famil-

iar with these laws, and learn to USE them. Through repetition, and by approaching the description of these principles from every conceivable angle, the author hopes to reveal to you the secret through which every great fortune has been accumulated. Strange and paradoxical as it may seem, the "secret" is NOT A SECRET. Nature, herself, advertises it in the earth on which we live, the stars, the planets suspended within our view, in the elements above and around us, in every blade of grass, and every form of life within our vision.

Nature advertises this "secret" in the terms of biology, in the conversion of a tiny cell, so small that it may be lost on the point of a pin, into the HUMAN BEING now reading this line. The conversion of desire into its physical equivalent is, certainly, no more miraculous!

You can derive confidence, faith, a renewed sense of self, and authentic help by placing yourself within the cyclical scheme of creation. This is the secret into which Hill's work invites you. Now, go and build.

APPENDIX A

Psychic Spies to the Rescue?

Ukraine's stunning destruction of a portion of Putin's air force on June 1, 2025, recalls an episode from the back pages of parapsychology and America's successful—yes, successful—CIA-funded psychic-spying program.

From about 1972 to 1995, the program, often called Project Stargate, employed "remote viewers" to attempt intelligence gets on foreign adversaries. In 1995, however, President Bill Clinton cut Stargate—funded at about $20 million across its run—in a spate of post-Cold War military reductions. There exists a popular shibboleth that Stargate failed to produce results. This is false.

In 2023, a team of social scientists endeavored to evaluate the remote-viewing [RV] program. They concluded in the journal *Brain and Behavior* that the chief thrust of Stargate—whose data was "progressively declassified" between 1995 and 2003—proved empirically sound: "In the case of RV [remote viewing], experiments with significant results greatly predominate."*

---

* Escolà-Gascón, Á., Houran, J., Dagnall, N., Drinkwater, K., & Denovan, A. (2023). Follow-up on the U.S. Central Intelligence Agency's (CIA) remote viewing experiments. *Brain and Behavior*, 13(6). https://doi.org/10.1002/brb3.3026

With apologies to Wikipedia, what I describe has proven so again and again since parapsychology commenced as an academic science nearly a century ago thanks to the efforts of researcher J.B. Rhine.

A further word about Ukraine before considering how this ties into Stargate and psychic spies. *The Wall Street Journal* reported on June 2, 2025:

> Ukraine's unprecedented drone strikes on Russian air force bases weaken Moscow's ability to wage war on its smaller neighbor and undermine its capacity to threaten more distant rivals such as the U.S.—a shift with potentially far-reaching geostrategic implications.
>
> A sizable portion of the fleet Moscow uses to launch guided-missile attacks on Ukraine—and would rely on to strike adversaries in the event of a nuclear war—was damaged or destroyed in the coordinated attacks.
>
> Russia no longer produces the decades-old Tupolev planes, meaning it has lost a cornerstone of its ability to project military power beyond its borders...
>
> Of more than 100 Tupolev bombers that Russia is known to have, Ukraine said it had damaged or destroyed more than 40.*

This resurrects a drama from Stargate. It is tucked away in a talk that former President Jimmy Carter delivered before a group of Emory University students in Atlanta in 1995—the same year Clinton cut the program. Carter's observation about psychic spy-

---

* "Ukraine's Stunning Assault Roils Russia's Global Military Strategy" by Daniel Michaels, *Wall Street Journal*, June 2, 2025.

ing appeared in a CNN news brief of September 21, 1995, which bears quoting in full:

> Carter: CIA used psychic to help find missing plane
>
> ATLANTA, Georgia (CNN)—Former President Jimmy Carter said the CIA, without his knowledge, once consulted a psychic to help locate a missing government plane in Africa. Carter told students at Emory University that the "special U.S. plane" crashed somewhere in Zaire while he was president.
>
> According to Carter, U.S. spy satellites could find no trace of the aircraft, so the CIA consulted a psychic from California. Carter said the woman "went into a trance and gave some latitude and longitude figures. We focused our satellite cameras on that point and the plane was there."
>
> Carter made the disclosure after two students asked if he was aware of any government evidence pointing to the existence of extraterrestrials. "I never knew of any instance where it was proven that any sort of vehicle had come from outer space to our country and either lived here or left," the former president said.

The plane to which Carter referred was, in fact, a *Soviet Tupolev-22 spy plane*, which crashed in Zaire in Central Africa in May 1978. The Tupolev was on an intelligence-gathering mission when it went down—providing a potential payload of Soviet intelligence technology.

Due to the coordinates and data supplied by remote viewers—which included a drawing of the tail of a plane emerging from a river—American reconnaissance and recovery teams were able to beat Soviet counterparts to the crash site, scoring a major intelligence victory. It ranked among Stargate's signature, if least-known, successes.

I currently have no knowledge of whether the intelligence gained in that episode contributed to Ukraine's ability to target Putin's aging but vital Tupolev fleet. But science has a funny way of summoning its truths beyond cultural vogue.

Among the reasons for Stargate's perceived discrediting are rhetorical assaults on the program by professional skeptic Ray Hyman dating to the program's demise in 1995. At the time, the later-president of the American Statistical Association, Jessica Utts—who uses statistical analysis and meta-analysis to study psi—cried foul on the skeptic. The two exchanged papers and rebuttals in 1995. But the signal got lost in the noise.*

Dean Radin, MS, PhD, chief scientist at the Institute of Noetic Sciences (IONS), and the scientist I consider Rhine's inheritor, notes:

> The American Institutes for Research (AIR) report that she and Hyman were consultants on was far more positive than it is typically portrayed. Both she and

---

* In 1995, Congress and the CIA commissioned Utts and University of Oregon psychologist Hyman to evaluate the results of Stargate. They produced counterpoint reports in 1995: "An Assessment of the Evidence for Psychic Functioning" by Jessica Utts, "Evaluation of a Program on Anomalous Mental Phenomena" by Ray Hyman, and "Response to Ray Hyman's Report of September 11, 1995" by Jessica Utts, which appear in full in both *Journal of Parapsychology*, 1995, Vol. 59, No. 4 and *Journal of Scientific Exploration*, 1996, Vol. 10, No. 1. The reports are further reprinted in *Journal of Parapsychology*, 2018, Vol. 82, Suppl. Utts' original report is rebutted by Hyman and she, in turn, responds to his rebuttal. For anyone interested in Stargate, I recommend this material amid a great deal of writing and debate on the matter.

> Hyman *agreed* that the evidence for RV was statistically significant and that its methodology was sound. The only sticking point was whether it was *useful* for espionage, and they actually didn't evaluate any of the operational missions data because they were classified (and most of it remains classified). Still, the AIR report said that RV wasn't useful, which contradicts [remote viewer] Joe McMoneagle's Legion of Merit award when he retired.

Wonderful strides have occurred in parapsychology, but the advances are not what they could be. In the same year as the Stargate cuts, UC Irvine statistician Jessica Utts, citing the work of Dutch researcher Sybo Schouten, surmised that during the more than 110 years since the founding of the Society for Psychical Research, "the total human and financial resources devoted to parapsychology since 1882 is at best equivalent to the expenditures devoted to fewer than two months of research in conventional psychology in the United States."*

For comparison, the American Psychological Association reports that in 2017, $2 billion of the United States' $66.5 billion in federal research funding went to psychological research. Think of it: the field of parapsychology has, since its inception worldwide, been funded in adjusted dollars at a rate of less than two months of traditional psychological experiments in the U.S. (experiments which, like much of the work in the social sciences, are routinely overturned to reflect changes or corrections in methodology). That is less than $333,500,000, or a little more than the cost of four fighter jets. This figure compares with trillions that

---

* From Utts' "Response to Ray Hyman's Report of September 11, 1995."

have been spent worldwide during the same period on physics or medical research.

Radin disputes my figure: "$333M is far too high. I'd estimate the total research dollars spent on psi research since 1882 is probably no more than $50M in today's dollars (including Stargate). That would pay for a small piece of one wing of a modern jet fighter."

Given the recent Tupolev drama and the fighter jet's place in the annals of Stargate, perhaps it is time for a second look.

APPENDIX B

Wild Talents: Why ESP Is Real*

> "All around are wild talents, and it occurs to nobody to try to cultivate them..."
> —Charles Fort, *Wild Talents*, 1932

I believe that our culture is poised for epochal change in how we understand and accept the core findings of parapsychology—that is, acceptance of the empiricism of the extraphysical.

Rejectionism tends to harden on the brink of seismic change, and we are seeing pockets of that as well. But the outcome of the present moment is, I believe, acknowledgment that we possess indelible evidence of an extraphysical component to life.

Formal scientific scrutiny of anomalous phenomena marked its starting point in 1882, when the Society for Psychical Research (SPR) was founded in London by scientists including F.W.H. Myers (who coined the term telepathy for mind-to-mind communication) and pioneering psychologist and philosopher William James.

---

* This essay originally appeared under the title "The Parapsychology Revolution" in the Winter 2023 issue of *Quest* magazine, published by the Theosophical Society in America. This version is expanded.

At its inception, parapsychology sought to test mediumistic phenomena under controlled conditions. The early SPR worked with rigor to hold spirit mediums to proof. Researchers such as the strong-willed Richard Hodgson and James himself ventured to the séance table intent on safeguarding against fraud and documenting claimed phenomena, including physical mediumship, after-death communication, and clairvoyance or what is today called channeling.

They probed unexplained cases, exposed frauds, and created historical controversies that have lingered until today. But they were working largely within the lace-curtained settings of Victorian parlors. On the whole, SPR researchers were not functioning in clinical environments, so-called white coat lab settings. The American chapter of the SPR, meanwhile, was stymied by factional disputes between members more interested in the after-death survival thesis and those committed to the more conservative direction of documenting mental phenomena.

I do not intend to leave the impression that lab-based study of psychical phenomena was absent. In the 1880s, Nobel laureate and SPR president Charles Richet, one of France's most highly regarded biologists, studied telepathy with subjects under hypnosis. Richet also introduced the use of statistical analysis in ESP card tests, presaging today's near-universal use of statistics throughout the psychological and social sciences. In the early 1920s, French engineer René Warcollier conducted a series of experiments on long-distance telepathy.

Sigmund Freud himself pondered the possibilities of telepathy, sometimes delaying publication of key statements posthumously to avoid professional fallout. This was the case with Freud's "Psychoanalysis and Telepathy," his earliest paper on the topic written in 1921—but withheld from publication until 1941, two years after his death. (This was likely at the urging of his English biographer Ernest Jones, who found the topic professionally compromising.)

The paranormal burgeoned into an acknowledged, if hotly debated, academic field thanks largely to ESP researcher J.B. Rhine (1895–1980) and his wife and intellectual partner Louisa Rhine (1891–1983). In the late 1920s and early '30s, the Rhines established the research program that became the Parapsychology Laboratory at Duke University in Durham, North Carolina, which made paradigmatic advances in the scientific study of ESP.

The Rhines trained as statisticians and botanists at the University of Chicago, where both received doctorates (a considerable rarity for a woman then). In Chicago in 1922, they were inspired by a talk on Spiritualism by English author Arthur Conan Doyle. With his eyes on greater horizons, J.B. soon grew restless in his chosen career.

"It would be unpardonable for the scientific world today to overlook evidences of the supernormal in our world," he told what must have been a mildly surprised audience of scientific agriculturalists at the University of West Virginia.

The Rhines began casting around, venturing to Columbia University and Harvard seeking opportunities to combine their scientific training with their metaphysical interests. Initial progress proved fitful. As often occurs in life, just before they gave up their immense efforts, an extraordinary opportunity appeared. In 1930, with the support of Duke's first president, William Preston Few, the new chairman of Duke's psychology department, William McDougall, made J.B. Rhine a formal part of the campus.

Although the founding of Duke's Parapsychology Laboratory is often dated to that year, the program was not christened the Parapsychology Laboratory until 1935, where it remained until

1965. Today the Rhine Research Center continues as an independent lab off campus. It proved a watershed episode in which parapsychology was formally folded into an academic structure and study of the psychical became a profession.

At Duke, J.B. Rhine did not quite originate but popularized the phrase extrasensory perception, or ESP, which soon became a household term. The work begun at Duke's Parapsychology Lab in the early 1930s has continued among different researchers, labs, and universities to the present day. The effort is to provide impeccably documented evidence that human beings participate in some form of existence that exceeds cognition, motor skill, and commonly observed biological functions—that we participate in trackable, replicable patterns of extra-physicality that permit us, at least sometimes, to communicate and receive information in a manner that surpasses generally acknowledged sensory experience and means of data conveyance. This field of exchange occurs independently of time, space, or mass.

We have also accumulated a body of statistical evidence for psychokinesis (i.e., mind over matter) and precognition or what is sometimes called retrocausality, in which events in the future affect the present. For several years, Dean Radin, chief scientist at the Institute of Noetic Sciences (IONS) in Northern California, has performed and replicated experiments in precognition in which subjects display bodily stressors, such as pupil dilation or increased heart rate, seconds before being shown distressing or emotionally triggering imagery.

These are fleeting references to a handful of recent findings from modern parapsychology. I am going to make a statement, and I am then going to argue for it: we possess heavily scrutinized, replicable statistical evidence for an extraphysical component of the human psyche. For decades, this evidence has appeared in—

and been reproduced for—traditional, academically based journals, often juried by scientists without sympathy for its findings. This evidence has been procured and replicated under rigorous clinical conditions. It demonstrates that the individual possesses or participates in a facet of existence that surpasses what is known to us biologically, psychologically, sensorily, and technologically. In short: ESP exists.

The search for greater dimensions of life is as old as humanity. But what is new and revolutionary is *the advent of science as a method of protocols to identify processes that affirm primordial humanity's basic instinct for the extraphysical.* As noted, this places our generation before a remarkable precipice. It is one that we have not yet been able to cross.

The precipice is the philosophy called materialism, by which Western life has organized itself for nearly three-hundred years. Philosophical materialism holds that matter creates itself, and that your mind is strictly epiphenomenal of your brain. Furthermore, thoughts are a localized function of gray matter which, like bubbles in a glass of carbonated water, are gone once the water is gone. And that is the extent of the psyche.

That philosophy is obsolete. Firstly, an enormous amount of data has amassed verifying both the perceptual basis of reality and extraphysicality—gathered through the same methodology that materialism purports to defend. Secondly, we face the progressing realization that materialism is simply a position, a theory, an ideology, of which science is independent.

This does not mean that materialism will fade gently. Its outlook—that matter evinces no calculable reality beyond classical mechanics and that all contrary evidence or implications are false because they contradict its founding premise—will retain influence for decades. The materialist perspective is concretized within key parts of our culture and media. Many opinion-shaping personalities hold to it with conviction.

What evidence exists for my claims of science affirming the infinite? Here I return to Duke's Parapsychology Laboratory in the early 1930s. Rhine's innovation as a researcher was developing clear, repeatable, and unimpeachable methods, with rigor and without drama or speculation, for testing and statistically mapping evidence for anomalous communication and conveyance. To attempt this, Rhine initially created a series of card-guessing tests that involved a deck called Zener cards designed by psychologist Karl E. Zener.

Zener cards are a five-suit deck, generally with twenty-five cards in a pack, with symbols that are easily and immediately recognizable: circle, square, cross, wavy lines, and five-pointed star. After a deck is shuffled, subjects are asked to attempt blind hits on what symbol will turn up. Probability dictates that if you are operating from random chance over large spreads, you are going to hit 20 percent, or one out of five. But Rhine discovered, across tens and eventually hundreds of thousands of rigorously safeguarded trials (by 1940, the database included nearly a million trials) that certain individuals, rather than scoring 20 percent, would score 25 percent, 26 percent, 27 percent, sometimes 28 percent (and in select cases a great deal higher).

At the time, social scientists commonly withheld negative sets of data on the questionable grounds that something was flawed with the methodology. Rhine reversed this practice early on at his lab and helped lead the overall social sciences to do so. All of the data were reported. Nothing was withheld in the file drawer. No negative sets were excluded. In Rhine's work, every precaution was taken against corruption, withholding, or pollution of data, which was also opened to other researchers (and non-research-based critics) for replication, vetting, and review.

In a letter of March 15, 1960, to mathematician and foundation executive Warren Weaver, Rhine spoke of the extra lengths to which the parapsychologist ought to go: "Even though the methodology and standards of evidence may compare favorably with other advances of natural science, they have to be superior in parapsychology because of its novelty; and conceivably, too, by making them still better, everything may be gained in overcoming the natural resistance involved."

The "natural resistance" or partisanship around such findings can be so intense—and sometimes purposefully obfuscating—that lay seekers may come away with the mistaken impression that Rhine's work, or that of more recent parapsychologists, has proven unrepeatable or compromised.

Parapsychologist Charles Honorton (1946–1992) sought to analyze critical challenges to Rhine's figures in the years following their publication. He found that "61 percent of the independent replications of the Duke work were statistically significant. This is 60 times the proportion of significant studies we would expect if the significant results were due to chance or error."

Rhine's experiments have proven so bulletproof that even close to fifty years later, his most resistant critics were still attempting to explain them by fantastical (and often feckless) fraud theories, including a prominent English skeptic's nearly vaudevillian supposition that one of the test subjects repeatedly crawled through a ceiling space to peek at cards through a trapdoor over the lab. At such excesses, rationalists fail the test that Enlightenment philosopher David Hume (1711–1772) set for validation of miracles: counterclaims must be less likely than reported phenomena. In any case, Rhine's methods and results have never been upended.

For all that, Rhine may have proved too idealistic regarding what it took to overcome "natural resistance." Mainstream media sources engage in pushback and even disingenuousness toward data from parapsychology. A prime example appears in how polemical skeptics today ride herd over articles on parapsychology on the most-read reference source in history, Wikipedia. As of this writing, Wikipedia's article on Zener cards states in its opening, "The original series of experiments have been discredited and replication has proven elusive." This statement is unsourced, something that would get red-flagged on most of the encyclopedia's articles.

How does this occur on the world's go-to reference source? Dean Radin of IONS described to me the problem of an ad hoc group calling itself "Guerilla Skeptics" policing Wiki entries on parapsychology: "While there are lots of anonymous trolls that have worked hard to trash any Wikipedia pages related to psi, including bios of parapsychologists, this group of extreme skeptics is proudly open that they are rewriting history . . . any attempt to edit those pages, even fixing individual words, is blocked or reverted almost instantly."

Even if parapsychology as a field had ended with Rhine's initial Duke trials, we would possess evidence of paranormal mechanics in human existence. Those basic (though painstakingly structured) card experiments, those few percentage points of deviation tracked across tens of thousands of trials (90,000 in the database by the 1934 publication of *Extra-Sensory Perception*), demonstrate an anomalous transfer of information in a laboratory setting and an extraphysical (call it metaphysical), non-Newtonian exchange of information.

But things did not end there. In the decades ahead, extraordinary waves of diversified experiments occurred in the U.S. and other nations growing from the efforts of the scientists at Duke's Parapsychology Laboratory. These efforts demonstrated, again and again, anomalous mental phenomena, including precognition, retrocausality, telepathy, and psychokinesis (PK).

Rhine's lab began studying PK in 1934, an effort that continued until 1941, after which many lab members were summoned to the war effort. During their nine years of investigation, researchers conducted tens of thousands of runs in which individuals would attempt to affect throws of random sets of dice. Devices were soon employed to toss the dice in such a way that ensured randomness, which ought to demonstrate no pattern whatsoever. Again, similar statistical results to the Zener card experiments appeared: among certain individuals, across hundreds of thousands of throws, with every conceivable safeguard, peer review, methodological transparency, and reportage of every set, there appeared a deviation of several percentage points, suggesting a physical effect arising from mental intention.

We have now logged generations of experiments designed to test the effects to which I am referring. Today's parapsychologists believe, I think with justification, that the basic, foundational science for psychical ability has already been laid. Although parapsychology remains controversial, the field has already moved on from basic testing for ESP, a matter that was more or less settled in the 1940s.

Recent researchers are concerned with questions including telepathy (mind-to-mind communication); precognition (the ability to foresee or be affected by things that, within our model of the mind, have not yet occurred); retrocausality (the effect of future events on current perceptions or abilities); a biological basis for psi (including biologist Rupert Sheldrake's morphic-field theories); spontaneous psi events, such as premonitions or crisis realizations; dream telepathy; a "global consciousness" effect during periods of mass emotional reaction; and the practice of remote viewing or clairvoyance. The field also investigates other important areas, including out-of-body experiences, near-death experiences, deathbed visions, after-death survival, and reincarnation.

Scientific study of reincarnation was pioneered as an academic field by the remarkable research psychiatrist Ian Stevenson (1918–2007), who founded the Division of Perceptual Studies at the University of Virginia. For five decades, this conservative researcher "traveled six continents, accumulating more than 2,500 cases of young children who recounted details of previous lives, which he meticulously verified with witnesses, hospital records, autopsy reports, death certificates, and photographs," eulogized the *Journal of Near-Death Studies* in Spring 2007.

One of the most important figures in psychical research died of heart failure in 1992 at the tragically young age of forty-six. I mentioned him earlier: his name is Charles Honorton. Honorton's passing was a tremendous loss for the field, nearly equivalent to losing Einstein at the dawn of his relativity theories.

It is critical to understand what Honorton accomplished. In the late 1960s and '70s, he engaged in direct research into dreams and ESP at the innovative Division of Parapsychology and Psychophysics at Maimonides Medical Center in Brooklyn. Honorton proceeded to assemble possibly the most significant body of data we possess in the parapsychology field. It was through a long-running series of experiments designed with colleagues in the 1970s and '80s known as *ganzfeld* experiments. Ganzfeld is German for whole or open field. Honorton had an instinct for the conditions under which ESP or telepathy—mind-to-mind communication—might be heightened, which formed the basis of his studies.

Honorton noted that the classic Rhine experiments were largely focused on subjects believed to have a predilection for

ESP. Rhine believed that ESP may be detectable throughout the human population but was readily testable through figures who possess innate abilities. He did not consider ESP something for which you could train or that was necessarily intrinsic to everyone. Rather, he focused on what he considered naturally gifted individuals, who made prime subjects. Honorton took a different tack. He wondered whether psychical abilities are, in fact, general throughout the population—but perhaps the psychical signal, so to speak, gets jammed or the psyche's circuitry gets overloaded due to excessive stimuli in daily life.

Honorton pondered what it might reveal to test for ESP among subjects who are placed into conditions of relaxed, comfortable sensory deprivation. He ventured that you may be able to spike the ESP effect if you place a subject into sensory-deprived conditions without noise or bright light—for example, seating the participant in a comfortable recliner in a dimly lit, noise-proof room or chamber, fitted with eyeshades, and wearing headphones that emit white noise. These conditions induce the state called *hypnagogia*, a kind of waking hypnosis.

In fact, you enter into the hypnagogic state twice daily: just before you drift to sleep at night and just as you are coming to in the morning. It is a deeply relaxed, motionless state in which you might experience hallucinatory or morphing images, aural hallucinations, tactile sensations of weightlessness, or even bodily paralysis. Yet you remain functionally awake: you are self-aware and able to direct cognition. The morning state is sometimes called *hypnopompia* (a term coined by psi research pioneer F.W.H. Myers). Hypnagogia and hypnopompia are similar with some differences; for example, hallucinations occur somewhat more commonly during the nighttime state.

Since this state is an apparently inviting period for self-suggestion—the mind is supple, the body relaxed, and the psyche unclouded by stimuli—Honorton pondered whether these conditions might facilitate heightened psychical activity. To test for telepathy, he placed one subject—called the receiver—into the relaxed conditions of sensory deprivation I have described, while a second subject—called the sender—is seated outside the sensory deprivation tank or in another space. In the classical ganzfeld experiments, the sender attempts to "transmit" a preselected image to the receiver. After the sending period ends, the receiver then chooses among four different images (one target image and three decoys) to identify what was sent.

Like the Zener cards, there is a randomly selected target on each successive trial and, in this case, a one in four or 25-percent chance of guessing right. In meta-analyzed data, subjects on average surpassed the 25-percent guess rate. Depending on the analytic model, the most stringently produced experiments demonstrated an overall hit rate of between 32 percent and 35 percent. Since the mid-1970s, this data has, in varying forms, been replicated by dozens of scientists across different labs in different nations, often under increasingly refined conditions. The ganzfeld experiments not only documented a significant psi effect but also suggested that a detectable ESP or telepathic effect may be more generally distributed among the population. The protocols themselves suggested conditions under which psi phenomena are most likely to appear.

Given its significance, the ganzfeld database attracted intense scrutiny. In a historic first, which has never really been repeated, Honorton in 1986 collaborated on a paper with a prominent psi skeptic, Ray Hyman, a professor of psychology at the University of Oregon. After trading written disputes over the validity of parapsychological experiments, the interlocutors decided to collaborate on a joint study for the *Journal of Parapsychology*, analyzing the data, highlighting areas of agreement and dispute, and recommending protocols for future experiments. In an arena where arguments often devolve into rhetoric, it proved a signature moment.

"Instead of continuing with another round of our debate on the psi ganzfeld experiments," they wrote, "we decided to collaborate on a joint communiqué. The Honorton-Hyman debate emphasized the differences in our positions, many of these being technical in nature. But during a recent discussion, we realized that we possessed similar viewpoints on many issues concerning parapsychological research. This communiqué, then, emphasizes these points of agreement."

In a joint statement—one that ought to serve as a general guardrail in our era of digital attack speech—Honorton and Hyman wrote: "Both critics and parapsychologists want parapsychological research to be conducted according to the best possible standards. The critic can contribute to this need only if his criticisms are informed, relevant, and responsible."

Beyond laying down general principles and research protocols, the collaborators conducted a joint meta-analysis of key ganzfeld experiments up to that moment. (A meta-analysis is a cumulative study of different but similar experiments to test pooled data for statistical significance.) "The data base analyzed by Hyman and Honorton," wrote UC Irvine statistician Jessica Utts, "consisted of results taken from 34 reports written by a total of 47 authors. Honorton counted 42 separate experiments described in the reports, of which 28 reported enough information to determine the number of direct hits achieved. Twenty three of the studies (55%) were classified by Honorton as having achieved statistical significance." The success rate was similar to Honorton's findings in his 1978 meta-analysis.

Notably, the psychical researcher and the skeptic wrote in their abstract: "We agree that there is an overall significant effect in this data base that cannot be reasonably explained by selective reporting or multiple analysis."

And further: "Although we probably still differ on the magnitude of the biases contributed by multiple testing, retrospective experiments, and the file-drawer problem, we agree that the overall significance observed in these studies cannot reasonably be explained by these selective factors. Something beyond selective reporting or inflated significance levels seems to be producing the nonchance outcomes. Moreover, we agree that the significant outcomes have been produced by a number of different investigators."

In sum, here was a key psychical researcher and a leading skeptic (Hyman was among the few skeptics who conducted his own research) disagreeing over the general nature of the ESP thesis—a reasonable disagreement—but affirming that the most important psychical data of the period proved unpolluted and that the methodology of the studies in their sample reflected significant improvement from the dawn of the experiments in the early to mid-1970s. But the key data, they wrote, was free from substantial error, corruption, or selective reporting. Hyman agreed that a statistically significant effect appears in the data and justifies further research. That's all. No concession of belief in ESP. Nor was any needed. Just an informed critique by a parapsychologist and a career-long skeptic, both with significant credentials, concluding that the data and practices are normative and a statistically significant anomaly appears.

It is tragic, both in terms of human pathos and intellectual advancement, that Honorton died six years after that paper was published. He was one of the only parapsychologists able to reach across the nearly unbridgeable partisan divide to a professional skeptic and create progress in dialogue and research. That process has never been repeated. Indeed, as of this writing, Wikipedia's article on the ganzfeld experiments introduces them as a "pseudoscientific technique," without sourcing.

It is worth asking why this chasm has remained so wide. Wonderful strides have occurred in parapsychology, but the advances are not what they could be. Statistician Jessica Utts, citing Dutch researcher Sybo Schouten, has noted that during the more than 110 years since the founding of the Society for Psychical Research, "the total human and financial resources devoted to parapsychology since 1882 is at best equivalent to the expenditures devoted to fewer than two months of research in conventional psychology in the United States."

For comparison, the American Psychological Association reports that in 2017, $2 billion of the United States' $66.5 billion in federal research funding went to psychological research.

Think of it: the field of parapsychology has, since its inception worldwide, been funded in adjusted dollars at a rate of less than two months of traditional psychological experiments in the U.S. (experiments which, like much of the work in the social sciences, are routinely overturned to reflect changes or corrections in methodology). That is less than $333,500,000, or a little more than the cost of four fighter jets. This figure compares with trillions that have been spent worldwide during the same period on physics or medical research.

As noted, Radin disputes my figure: "$333M is far too high. I'd estimate the total research dollars spent on psi research since 1882 is probably no more than $50M in today's dollars (including Stargate). That would pay for a small piece of one wing of a modern jet fighter." The CIA's Project Stargate is considered in Appendix A.

This funding situation reflects, in part, the success of the most vociferous skeptics in disabling the legitimacy of parapsychological data. Most academic researchers steer clear, fearing damage to their reputation and ability to get other projects funded.

Even in this atmosphere, however, some scientists prevail against the tide. A historic episode occurred in 2011, which marked the publication of a paper called "Feeling the Future" by well-known research psychologist Daryl J. Bem of Cornell University. For about ten years, Bem conducted a series of nine experiments involving more than 1,000 participants into precognition or "time reversing" of widely established cognitive or psychological effects, such as memorization of a list or responding to negative or erotic stimuli flashed as images on a screen. Bem's discoveries demonstrated the capacity of cognition across boundaries of linear time.

Bem, like other researchers including Dean Radin, identified factors that seem to correlate with precognition, such as the body's response to arousing or disturbing imagery. As Bem wrote of previous experiments: "Most of the pictures were emotionally neutral, but a highly arousing negative or erotic image was displayed on randomly selected trials. As expected, strong emotional arousal occurred when these images appeared on the screen, but the remarkable finding is that the increased arousal was observed to occur a few seconds before the picture appeared, before the computer had even selected the picture to be displayed."

In one of Bem's trials, subjects were asked to "guess" at erotic images alternated with benign images. "Across all 100 sessions," he wrote, "participants correctly identified the future position of the erotic pictures significantly more frequently than the 50% hit rate expected by chance: 53.1%... In contrast, their hit rate on the nonerotic pictures did not differ significantly from chance:

49.8%... This was true across all types of nonerotic pictures: neutral pictures, 49.6%; negative pictures, 51.3%; positive pictures, 49.4%; and romantic but nonerotic pictures, 50.2%."

The response to either arousing or disturbing imagery is suggestive of the emotional stakes required for the presence of a psi effect. Stakes must exist, and strong emotions must be in play. Passion is critical. In his 1937 *New Frontiers of the Mind*, Rhine emphasized the role of spontaneity, confidence, comity, novelty, curiosity, and lack of fatigue. (And, as it happens, caffeine.)

But Bem's horizons extended further. In the most innovative element of his nine-part study, he set out to discover whether subjects displayed improved recall of lists of words that were to be practice-memorized in the future. In Bem's words, "whether rehearsing a set of words makes them easier to recall—even if the rehearsal takes place after the recall test is given."

Participants were first shown a set of words and given a free recall test of those words. They were then given a set of practice exercises on a randomly selected subset of those words. The psi hypothesis was that the practice exercises would retroactively facilitate the recall of those words, and, hence, participants would recall more of the to-be-practiced words than the unpracticed words. Bem found a statistically significant improvement of recall on the lists of words studied in the near future: "The results show that practicing a set of words after the recall test does, in fact, reach back in time to facilitate the recall of those words." In short, future memorization heightened current recall.

Unsurprisingly, Bem's 2011 paper met with tremendous controversy. Within a year of Bem's publication, a trio of professional skeptics published a rejoinder. Playing off of Bem's "Feeling the Future," their paper sported the media-friendly title, "Failing the Future." The experimenters reran one of Bem's experiments. They concluded, "All three replication attempts failed to produce significant effects... and thus do not support the existence of psychic ability."

But the authors omitted a critical detail from their own database. By deadline, they possessed two independent studies that validated Bem's results. They made no mention of these studies, despite their own ground rules for doing so. Bem wrote in his response: "By the deadline, six studies attempting to replicate the Retroactive Recall effect had been completed, including the three failed replications reported by Ritchie et al. and two other replications, *both of which successfully reproduced my original findings at statistically significant levels*... Even though both successful studies were pre-registered on Wiseman's registry and their results presumably known to Ritchie et al., they fail to mention them in this article." (emphasis added)

Although there unquestionably exists a significant crisis of replicability and data manipulation—not to mention fraud—in the sciences, no one has tied any of this to Bem or his methods. As of July 2020, Bem's experiments (including the original trials) proved confirmatory in a meta-analysis encompassing 90 experiments in 33 laboratories in 14 countries, "greatly exceeding" the standard for "'decisive evidence' in support of the experimental hypothesis," as Bem and his coauthors wrote in the abstract of their follow-up paper.

I believe that I am highlighting only the glacial tip of how parapsychological data is misreported within much of mainstream news media and large swaths of academia. The question returns: why? I have difficulty understanding human nature, which is, finally, the crux of the matter. After a certain point of tautological criticism of nearly a century of academic ESP research, it becomes difficult to avoid using a strong word that I prefer not to use and that I do not use lightly: suppression. Not of any centrally organized sort, but of a cultural sort in which prevailing findings run so counter to materialist assumptions that critics—who ironically perceive themselves as arbiters of rationality—assume an "at any cost" stance to dispel contrary data. Winning becomes more important than proving. It is the antithesis of science. This is the irony to which professional skepticism has brought us.

This kind of practice—in which self-perceived rationalists do injustice to truth in pursuit of what they consider a defense of rationalism—has run riot throughout the professional skeptics' field. Cambridge biologist Rupert Sheldrake, in addition to his own research into psi phenomena, has proven determined and intrepid in responding to serial problems among professional skeptics and the toll they have taken in reference media and journalism. Sheldrake was named one of the top 100 Global Thought Leaders of the year by Switzerland's prestigious Duttweiler Institute. Yet today on Wikipedia he is called a purveyor of "pseudoscience" for his theories of biological resonance and psi.

I have already mentioned earlier that the social and natural sciences are experiencing a credibility gap. One study has suggested that fraud rates in biomedical and psychology research are probably at a respective 9 percent and 10 percent. I consider it defensible to state that parapsychology today may be among the few exceptions to common fraud in the social sciences.

When I posted about the matter in late 2021 on social media, parapsychology journalist Craig Weiler put it this way:

> Because parapsychology doesn't convey any honors from successful research, either through social acknowledgment or an improvement in professional status, there is little motivation for cheating. Successful

studies also have to run the skeptical gauntlet. So, little incentive... Just a personal observation, the field seems to attract uncorruptible people. The people who take it seriously and publicly, have to have a generally reduced fear level and be willing to fight for the importance of truth. That doesn't describe your average cheater.

Indeed, it is infinitely more important to me as an advocate of parapsychology research that we get it right versus win a debate. I would rather lose ground a hundred times over than proffer an argument that is strictly rhetorical or tactical in nature or that misrepresents key findings when a debate goes against me. That is why I am so flummoxed (perhaps naively) when I encounter self-described skeptics who use deceptive or slippery methods in the interest of promulgating intellectual soundness.

In some regards, what I detect among ideological skeptics is a general facet of human nature. For most people, data that challenges self-conception or confidence of position, is not so much weighed and rejected as *not sensed*. This is what spiritual philosopher G.I. Gurdjieff (1866–1949) termed a "buffer"—a psychological protector that keeps contrary or self-revealing impressions from entering the psyche, in the most literal sense.

The point of query is not prevailing, or even proving, but searching—honoring the basic human question of what lies around the next hill. In 2025, I gave an hour-long interview to a television producer writing a popular book on anomalous phenomena. "I don't know if you're gonna like the book," he later told me. "Because I debunk certain things around ESP." It was clear that he had not taken in the substance of what I had said—again, a "buffer."

Neither I nor any reputable parapsychologist wishes to dictate outcome but rather foster greater academic and intellectual leeway so that scientists probing anomalous cognition need not fear damage to career or reputation. As noted, psi research is inexpensive. Because the skeptics have proven so successful, however, most parapsychologists today must secure independent funding. Anyone who has written grant proposals knows that that process is the equivalent of a job in itself. But the men and women who populate parapsychology today carry out this labor while also conducting their research and often holding academic or clinical positions to pay the bills. What's more, they often endure professional insults and calumny.

I recognize that skeptics fear a wave of irrationality will be unleashed on the world if headlines start announcing, "Harvard Study Says ESP Is Real." Consequently, they strive against that day (although in various forms it has already come and gone), just as in an exchange with Sigmund Freud, his English disciple Ernest Jones protested that acknowledging telepathy "would mean admitting the essential claim of the occultists that mental processes can be independent of the human body."

The issues I am describing have easily cost us more than a generation of progress in parapsychology. We are at least thirty or forty years behind where we ought to be, dated from when the professional skeptical apparatus began to ramp up in the mid-1970s.

One real challenge for parapsychology—and addressing this is, I think, necessary to the field's next leap forward—is to arrive at a theory of conveyance. I believe the field needs a persuasive theoretical model that pulls together the effects and posits how information is transferred in a manner unbound by time, space, distance, linearity, and common sensory experience. Researchers have made preliminary steps in this direction. Advances are overdue.

In 1960, Warren Weaver, a highly regarded mathematical engineer and grant-making science foundation executive, uttered a semi-famous lament about ESP research at a panel discussion at Dartmouth College: "I find this whole field [parapsychology] intellectually a very painful one. And I find it painful essentially for the following reasons: I cannot reject the evidence and I cannot accept the conclusions." Weaver caught hell for his statement; some colleagues questioned whether his judgment had slipped; a few others (including Dartmouth's president) privately thanked him for broaching the topic.

Weaver had toured Rhine's labs in early 1960. On February 22, he privately wrote Rhine to raise several issues. Near the top of his seven-page, singled-spaced letter, Weaver made this point: "For if you could make substantial progress in analyzing, explaining, and controlling, then the problem of acceptance would be largely solved." Rhine had long labored to demonstrate effect, Weaver wrote, but he now needed to describe mechanics. His letter continued:

> But for three main reasons—or at least so it seems to me—the problem of acceptance remains. First, these phenomena are so strange, so outside the normal framework of scientific understanding, that they are inherently very difficult to accept. Second, the attempts to analyze, understand, and control have not been, as yet, very successful or convincing. And third, unreasonable and stubborn as it doubtless appears to you, very many scientists are not convinced by the evidence which you consider is more than sufficient to establish the reality of the psi phenomena.

Rhine replied:

> The three main reasons you give in your analysis are recognizably correct. Had you been inclined at this point to go a step further into the intellectual background for these reasons, this might have been the point to draw upon the judgments of some of the philosophers and other commentators who have dealt with the problem of acceptance. There is an increasingly candid recognition of the difficulty as an essentially metaphysical one. Psi phenomena appear to challenge the assumption of a physicalistic universe.

Rhine was reluctant to draw theoretical conclusions from his findings. As his daughter, Sally Rhine Feather, wrote in a private communication to me: "I have never known him to have gone very far in this direction... But he was always so cautious at going beyond the data and had this aversion to philosophers who did so—except for the implications of the nonphysical nature of psi on which he actually speculated extremely broadly at times." She went on to quote from his 1953 book *New World of the Mind*: "It will be the task of biophysics and psychophysics to find out if there are unknown, imperceptible, extraphysical influences in nature that function in life and mind, influences which can interact with detectable physical processes."

In his response to Weaver, Rhine was referencing commonly accepted physical laws at the time. For psychical researchers today, studies in quantum theory, retrocausality, extra-dimensionality, neuroplasticity, string theory, and "morphic fields" that enable communication at the cellular level (the innovation of Rupert

Sheldrake) suggest a set of physical laws that surpass the known and may serve as a kind of macroverse within which familiar mechanics are experienced. It was already clear in Rhine's era that extrasensory transmission could not be explained through a "mental radio" model, since, according to Rhine's tests and those of others, ESP is unaffected by time, distance, or physical barriers.

This returns us to the question: If the psi effect is real, how does it work? How does mentality exceed the obvious boundaries of sensory transmission?

Perhaps science overvalues theory. Nonetheless, I believe that it falls to each generation to venture a theory of phenomena in which it professes deep interest. That theory can ignite a debate—it can be thrown out and replaced, it can be modified—but I do not believe that researchers and motivated lay inquirers (like me) can eschew the task. For this reason, I attempted a theory of mind causation in the closing chapter of my 2018 book *The Miracle Club* entitled, "Why It Works."

Consider this: when you say the word precognition, it strikes many people as fantastical, as though we are entering crystal-ball territory. Why the incredulity? We already know, and have known for generations, that linear time as we experience it is an illusion. Einstein's theories of relativity, and experiments that have affirmed them, establish that time slows in conditions of extreme velocity—at or approaching lightspeed—and in conditions of extreme gravity, like black holes. The individual traveling in a metaphorical spaceship at or near lightspeed experiences time slowing (not from their perspective but in comparison to those not at that speed), and this is not a mere thought exercise. Space travelers in our era, although they are obviously approaching nowhere near that velocity, experience minute reductions in aging.

In short, linear time is a *necessary illusion* for five-sensory beings to get through life. Time is not an absolute. What's more, ninety years of work in quantum physics leads us to theorize that we face an infinitude of concurrent realities—not as possibility but as logical necessity—one of which we will localize or experience within our framework based upon perspective or when we look.

To switch tacks, string theory posits that all of reality is interconnected by vast networks of vibrating strings. Everything, from the tiniest particle to entire universes to other dimensions, is linked by these undulating strings. Hence something that occurs within another dimension not only affects what happens in the reality of the dimension that we occupy but signals an infinitude of events playing out in these other fields of existence, as in ours.

We may even crisscross into these concurrent realities, occupying lives that are infinite in terms of the psyche and variable in dimensional occupancy. Experiencing data or events from other dimensions may also be extrapolated to UFO encounters or other anomalous phenomena.

Perhaps an individual, either because he or she is uniquely sensitive at a given moment or experiences a reduction of sensory data while retaining awareness (as in the ganzfeld experiments), is capable of accessing information—or taking measurements—from other states or dimensions that exist along the theorized bands of strings.

We call these measurements precognition, telepathy, ESP, or psychokinesis, the last of which may be a form of pre-awareness or movement or both. But maybe that is simply *what finer measurement looks like*. It is possible that measurement not only informs but also (at least in certain cases) actualizes, localizes, and determines. *Measurement selects*. Perhaps if we gleaned what was actually going on, or exercised fuller capacities of sensation, the experience would prove overwhelming. We would be overcome with data. Hence we may need a linear sense of time and a limited field of information in order to *navigate experience.*

Our linear, cause-and-effect sense of reality is already subverted by findings from quantum-computing prototypes—indeed the explanation for anomalous cognition may not arise from parapsychology but from adjacent theorizing in the computational field. In that vein, let me return to an observation on which this book began. On December 9, 2024, Google issued this statement noted earlier about a trial-run of its quantum-computing processor Willow:

> Willow's performance on this benchmark is astonishing: It performed a computation in under five minutes that would take one of today's fastest supercomputers 10^{25} or 10 septillion years. If you want to write it out, it's 10,000,000,000,000,000,000,000,000 years. This mind-boggling number exceeds known timescales in physics and vastly exceeds the age of the universe. It lends credence to the notion that quantum computation occurs in many parallel universes, in line with the idea that we live in a multiverse, a prediction first made by David Deutsch.

The social prejudices that dominate activist skepticism, as well as the philosophical materialism that governs much of the social sciences and humanities*, do not necessarily translate to computer engineering and finance, fields now experimenting with

---

* E.g., see my "Question Authorities: How the Social Sciences Pathologize Belief in the Paranormal," Substack, May 6, 2025.

APPENDIX B: WILD TALENTS: WHY ESP IS REAL 205

practical launches of quantum computing. These disciplines are acknowledging theses about our quantum universe in matters of both computation and cognition. It is time for seeking individuals, including readers of this essay, to do the same.

As suggested, not all members of our generation are comfortable with—or capable of—making this leap. Permit me a byway that revisits the "buffer" question. After I described the Willow data on a 2025 podcast, a viewer clapped back:

@BullyMaguire4ever 12 days ago (edited)
He is misrepresenting the quantum computer news. The headline on it was a misunderstanding. They didn't find that at all.

What the quantum computer did is solve an equation that would take the previously most power supercomputer longer than the age of the universe to solve. It doesn't imply multiverse, it implies that the quantum computer is very powerful and orders of magnitude faster.

👍 👎   Reply

@mitchhorowitz6054 6 minutes ago (edited)
I am sorry but that's incorrect. Here are the facts directly quoted, no "misrepresentation" or "headline," from Google engineers on December 9, 2024: "Willow's performance on this benchmark is astonishing: It performed a computation in under five minutes that would take one of today's fastest supercomputers 10^25 or 10 septillion years. If you want to write it out, it's 10,000,000,000,000,000,000,000,000 years. This mind-boggling number exceeds known timescales in physics and vastly exceeds the age of the universe. It lends credence to the notion that quantum computation occurs in many parallel universes, in line with the idea that we live in a multiverse, a prediction first made by David Deutsch [E.g., The Fabric of Reality: The Science of Parallel Universes—and Its Implications (1997)]" (Neven, H., 2024, December 9, "Meet willow, our state-of-the-art quantum chip." Google.)

You can, I believe, detect in this comment inability to perceive data in conflict with self-avowed verities. This human malady, more so than data and theories, render reality a receding horizon line. Nobel Prize winner in physics Max Planck (1858–1947) observed: "A new scientific truth does not triumph by convincing its opponents and making them see the light, but rather because its opponents eventually die, and a new generation grows up that is familiar with it." (As a coda, and for who-knows-what reason, my reply was removed from YouTube.)

And yet: given that we understand spacetime as flexible, is it really so strange, so violative of our current body of knowledge, that there exist quantifiable exceptions to ordinary sensory experience? As we document these exceptions, trace their arc, and replicate the conditions under which they occur, perhaps we approach what poet and mystic William Blake foresaw in 1790 in

The Marriage of Heaven and Hell: "If the doors of perception were cleansed every thing would appear to man as it is: Infinite." And thus ineffable.

In closing, I posit Seven Laws of Parapsychology:
1. Information exchange occurs outside common sensory experience or known technology.
2. This exchange occurs beyond classical boundaries of mass, space, or linearity.
3. Cognitive events in the perceived future are backwardly causative in the perceived present—or retrocausal.
4. Retrocausality is governed by quantum mechanics not by the "arrow of time" or second law of thermodynamics.
5. Hypnagogia or sensory deprivation heightens extrasensory exchange.
6. The aforementioned effects are replicable throughout the population though variable by individual.
7. The aforementioned effects are non-violative of special relativity or quantum mechanics, notwithstanding contradictions between both.

APPENDIX C

The 30-Day Mental Challenge

This little piece has generated more testimonials and requests than any I have ever written. I include one of special poignance at the end. From my experience and that of myriad seekers: The 30-Day Mental Challenge works. Try it.

* * *

American philosopher William James (1842–1910) yearned to find a practical spirituality, one that produced concrete improvements in happiness.

The Harvard physician grew encouraged, especially in his final years, by his personal experiments with New Thought, which in his 1902 *The Varieties of Religious Experience* he called "the religion of healthy-mindedness." I challenge today's seekers to continue James's search for a testable, workable spiritual system. Will you attempt a 30-day experiment that puts positive-mind metaphysics to the test?

The experiment is based on a passage from a 1931 book, *Body, Mind, and Spirit* by Elwood Worcester and Samuel McComb. The authors, both Episcopal ministers, in 1906 founded the Emmanuel Movement, a respected healing ministry popular in the early twentieth century. The Emmanuel Movement was named for Emmanuel Church in Boston's Back Bay. Worcester and McComb, joint pastors of the church, drew together ministers, physicians, psychologists, and patients to study and apply the regenerative abilities of the mind.

They collaborated with mainstream scientists, the most remarkable of which was Harvard physician and researcher Richard C. Cabot (1868–1939), who acted as Emmanuel's chief medical adviser. Cabot aimed to wed the possibilities of mind-power to scientific rationalism, and thus devise a mental therapeutics that could win allies among medical authorities.

In *Body, Mind, and Spirit*, a prominent scientist, who the authors did not name, told a small audience how he radically improved his life through a one-month thought experiment. I have condensed his testimony:

> Up to my fiftieth year I was unhappy, ineffective, and obscure. I had read some New Thought literature and some statements of William James on directing one's attention to what is good and useful and ignoring the rest. Such ideas seemed like bunk—but feeling that life was intolerable I determined to subject them to a month-long test.
>
> During this time, I resolved to impose definite restrictions on my thoughts. In thinking of the past, I would dwell only on its pleasing incidents. In thinking of the present, I would direct attention to its desirable elements. In thinking of the future, I would regard every worthy and possible ambition as within reach.

I threw myself into this experiment. I was soon surprised to feel happy and contented. But the outward changes astonished me more. I deeply craved the recognition of certain eminent men.

The foremost of these wrote me, out of the blue, inviting me to become his assistant. All my books were published. My colleagues grew helpful and cooperative.

It seems that I stumbled upon a *path of life*, and set forces working for me which were previously working against me.

Let's repeat this experiment together: 1) Choose your start date, 2) write out the full quoted passage above by hand (never underestimate the value of that), and 3) add: "I dedicate myself on this day of _____ to focus on all that is nourishing, advancing, and promising for thirty days (signed) "

That's it.

I suggest writing this passage on an index card (albeit a large one) and on the reverse creating a grid in which you mark off each of your thirty days. I advise rereading the scientist's testimony each morning and each time you mark off a day, as well as whenever it feels necessary.

You may want to carry your statement with you during the day. Whenever you find yourself sliding into old habits of thought, do not worry; simply steer back to the experiment. You do not need to start over. Just carry on.

* * *

The following testimonial appears with the correspondent's permission.

A debt of gratitude

Fri, Mar 28, 2025

Dear Mitch,

This is a thank-you letter. Last year I took up your 30-Day challenge. I was at the time 52, a college professor, but my career was not going well. I felt like I needed to make a change, but I had tried several times, with no success. My salary had not increased in a great while, and would sometimes fluctuate, if a class was under-enrolled and canceled. As a result, I was living with roommates, people I did not know, and I had moved 4 times in 2 years.

I began the 30-day challenge, and in addition I used the technique (described in *Daydream Believer*) of making a wish. I wished for "enough money" and a comfortable place to live within six months.

By the end of six months I had found a comfortable place to rent and a new job, albeit part-time, but at a much more prestigious university, one at which I had in the past dreamt of teaching. Then late last year I received a better contract from that same university, almost twice as much, for the Winter semester. Then the biggest surprise came in February: HR at the university said "Given your duties, you are full time: please sign this new contract." With the new contract came another bump in pay. I also now have time for writing. On the scholarly side this summer, I will be giving two papers at two different conferences.

Thank you so much for this 30-Day challenge as well as sharing your methods of making a wish in *Daydream Believer*.

I hope you are well.

Best regards,
Daniel

Index

A

Abrams, J. J., 69
acquisitiveness, 44, 166
Adorno, Theodor W., 101
affirmations / mantras, 17,
   22–27, 28–29, 32, 34–35, 37
aging process, 166–167
AI (artificial intelligence), 13
Alcoholics Anonymous (AA),
   28
Alfred P. Sloan Foundation, 12
Alien Encounters (Discovery /
   HBO Max show), 69, 70
Al-Kemi (Vanden Broeck),
   101–102
American Association for the
   Advancement of Science
   (AAAS), 12
   "Quantum Retrocausation"
   conference, 114–116
American Institute of Physics
   (AIP), 114–115
American Institutes of Research
   (AIR), 176–177

The American Newness (Howe),
   102
American Psychological
   Association (APA), 148,
   177–178, 193
American Psychologist (journal),
   148
American Statistical
   Association, 176
Amiel, Henri-Frédéric, 80
Andersen, U. S. (Uell Stanley
   Andersen), *Three Magic
   Words* (formerly *The Key to
   Power and Personal Peace*), 39
animal magnetism (Mesmer),
   44, 45
"astral light" (Lévi), 44–46
Authors of the Impossible
   (Kripalmy), 59
autosuggestion, 21–38, 189–190
   Émile Coué and, 22–24, 33–35
   Napoleon Hill and, 21–22
   hypnotism and, 23
   Maxwell Maltz and, 22, 35–38

autosuggestion (*cont.*)
  R.H.J. and, 31–32, 33
  self-image and, 21–25, 35–38
Aykroyd, Dan, 69–70

B

Baby Girl (2024 film), 65
backwards causation. *see* retrocausality
Baphomet, 47
The Beatles, 22–23, 27
"Beautiful Boy" (song), 27
Behrend, Genevieve, 161, 164
  Your Invisible Power, 158–159
Bem, Daryl J., 102–107, 108, 122–123, 148, 194–196
Better Call Saul (TV program) 1, 114
Beyond Good and Evil (Nietzsche), 113
Beyond UFOs and the Unknown (2024 docuseries), 69
Blake, William, *The Marriage of Heaven and Hell*, 205–206
Blavatsky, Madame H. P., 18–19
Bob Taylor's Magazine, 153–154
Body, Mind, and Spirit (Worcester and McComb), 207–209
The Book of the Law (Crowley), 53
Bradley, Ed, 75
Brain and Behavior (journal), 10, 15, 173
Bristol, Claude M., 131–151
  The Magic of Believing, 131–133, 136, 139–140, 141–142, 143–147, 149–150, 151
  The Magic of Believing for Young People, 151
  money passion and, 133–139, 149
  Shriner's Hospital for Crippled Children and, 140–141
  T.N.T., 134–139, 151
  World War I military service, 132–133, 136
Bristol, Edith, 140–141
Brooks, David, 64
Buddhism, 113
Bulwer-Lytton, Edward, *Vril: The Power of the Coming Race*, 44
Burroughs, William S., 52

C

Cabot, Richard C., 208
caffeine, 16, 195
Cane, Mike, 144
Cardeña, Etzel, 148
Carlisle, Belinda, 109
Carnegie, Andrew, 153–156
  "The Gospel of Wealth" (formerly "Wealth"), 154–156
  Homestead Strike (1892) and, 155
  philanthropy and, 156
Carter, Jimmy, 174–175
Castel, Jacqueline, 24, 69, 134
Castel, Jean-Gabriel, 24
Cayce, Edgar, 49
Central Intelligence Agency (CIA), Project Stargate, 10, 62, 173–178, 193
Cheel, Jay, 69

Chopra, Deepak, 142
Chronicles: Volume One (Dylan), 75
clairvoyance / channeling, 9–10, 180, 187–188
Clinton, Bill, 173, 174–175
Cognitive Behavioral Therapy (CBT), 40–41
Columbia University, 181
The Conduct of Life (Emerson), 137
confirmation bias, 11, 70
Constant, Alphonse-Louis, 44
Cornell University, 148
Cosmic Habit Force (Hill), 158, 159–160, 169–170
Coué, Émile, 22–35
  autosuggestion and, 22–24, 33–35
  "day by day" mantra, 17, 22–27, 28, 32, 34–35
  hypnotism and, 23
  influence of, 27–33
  lecture tour in the U.S., 31–33
  My Method, Including American Impressions, 32–33
  Psycho-Cybernetics and, 35, 41
  Self Mastery Through Conscious Autosuggestion, 23–24, 34–35
Covey, Edward, 89–90
Crowley, Aleister, 44
  The Book of the Law, 53

D

Dalí, Salvador, 25, 35
The Dark Half (King), 126
Dartmouth College, 200
Daydream Believer (Horowitz), 78, 210
Definite Chief Aim (DCA, Hill), 10, 11–13, 69, 70–71, 97, 129–130, 133, 149
The Denver Post, 132–133
Deutsch, David, 14, 14n
Deutsch, L. D., 114
Dey, Frederick Van Rensselaer, *The Magic Story*, 127–128, 129
Dey, Haryot Holt, 128
Dianetics (Hubbard), 39
Diller, Phyllis, 143, 144
D'Intino, Antonio, 70
Diotima, 48
Doctrine and Ritual of High Magic (Lévi), 45, 75–76
Doermann, Robin, 122–123
Douglass, Frederick, 88–90, 91, 93
Doyle, Arthur Conan
  "The Adventures of the Copper Beeches," 26
  Spiritualism, 181
dress
  dual self and, 128
  success and, 135–136
Driscoll, J. Walter, 56
dual self, 125–130
  divine hermaphrodites, 125
  Jekyll-Hyde, 126–127
  meeting, 128–130
  plus-entity (Dey), 127–128, 129
  shadow, 126
Duke University, Parapsychology Laboratory / Rhine Research Center, 9, 11–13, 16–17, 147–148,

181–182, 184–187, 188–189, 200–202
Dylan, Bob, *Chronicles: Volume One*, 75

E
Einstein, Albert, 103, 116, 202
Emerson, Ralph Waldo, 137–139
  The Conduct of Life, 137
  "History," 157
  "Over-Soul," 157
  Power, 137–138
  self-help as term and, 137
  Wealth, 137, 138–139
Emmanuel Church (Boston), 208
Emmanuel Movement, 207–208
entropy, 114, 117–118
Erikson, Leif, 67
Eros, 48, 51
Erotic Crystallization Inertia (ECI), 65
ersatz communication, as predatory behavior, 86
esoteric theology, 44, 100, 101, 106–107, 157
ESP (extrasensory perception), 179–206
  believers *vs.* nonbelievers in, 10, 11–13, 15, 17, 30–31, 186, 188–193, 197–199
  funding for research, 193–194
  hypnagogia and, 30
  as term, 9, 182
  Zener cards, 11–12, 16, 180, 184, 186, 187, 190
  see also clairvoyance / channeling; parapsychology; precognition; psychokinesis; remote viewing; retrocausality; telepathy
Everett, Hugh, III, 14n
Extraordinary Evidence: ESP Is Real (podcast), 69
Extrasensory Perception (Rhine), 16, 186

F
Faust (Goethe), 66
Feather, Sally Rhine, 201
Few, William Preston, 181
Feynman, Richard, 118–119, 121
Flashman (Fraser), 83
Fonda, Jane, 35
Formulae of Zos Vel Thanatos (Spare), 60
Fort, Charles, *Wild Talents*, 179
Fraser, George MacDonald, *Flashman*, 83
The Free Press, 58, 60
Freud, Sigmund, 180–181, 199

G
Gandhi, Mahatma, 63, 135–136
ganzfeld experiments, 30–31, 188, 190–193, 203
Garvey, Marcus, 32
genii, 51–52
"Getting Better" (song), 27
ghosting, as predatory behavior, 86–87
Global Consciousness Project, 148
Global Thought Leaders, 197
Gnosticism, 47

Goddard, Neville, 13, 18, 30, 110–113, 116–121, 162
Goethe, Johann Wolfgang von, *Faust*, 66
"The Gospel of Wealth" (formerly "Wealth," Carnegie), 154–156
Great Depression, 139
Great Recession (2008), 76
Greer, John Michael, 45
Grierson, Bruce, 167n
Gurdjieff, G. I., 29, 56, 77–79, 198
  Meetings with Remarkable Men, 97–99
Gurdjieff International Review (journal), 56

H
hallucinations, 189
Hanley, Spencer, 107–109
Hare Krishna, 94
Harvard Medical School, 27–28
Harvard University, 181
hate, love and, 112
Hermeticism, 52, 101, 157
Hermitage House, 39
Hill, Napoleon, 12, 43–53, 131, 166, 168
  autosuggestion and, 21–22
  at *Bob Taylor's Magazine*, 153–154
  Andrew Carnegie and, 153–154
  Cosmic Habit Force and, 158, 159–160, 169–170
  Definite Chief Aim (DCA) and, 10, 11–13, 69, 70–71, 97, 129–130, 133, 149
  Infinite Intelligence and, 14–15, 52, 157–158, 160–161
  "Invisible Counselors" and, 18–19
  The Law of Success, 76, 153
  The Master Key to Riches, 81
  Master Mind groups, 77, 169
  perseverance and, 97
  "secret" of, 169–171
  sex transmutation and, 43–44, 47–53
  Think and Grow Rich, 9, 14–15, 16, 21, 39–40, 43, 48–49, 59, 68, 126–127, 153, 169–171
Hinduism, 94, 113
Hodgson, Richard, 180
Homestead Strike (1892), 155
Honorton, Charles, 30, 185, 188–193
Horowitz, Mitch, 123–124
  Alien Encounters (TV program) and, 69, 70
  becomes a writer, 67–68, 73, 90, 141, 165, 167–168
  breaks into television and movies, 68–70
  Daydream Believer (2022), 78, 210
  as editor at The Free Press, 58, 60
  as editor at Penguin Random House, 35–36, 45, 60, 76, 165
  education, 167
  Extraordinary Evidence podcast and, 69

Horowitz, Mitch (*cont.*)
  family background, 165
  The Magic of Believing (Bristol) and, 145–147
  The Miracle Club (2018), 202
  The Miracle of a Definite Chief Aim (2019), 10, 11–13
  Occult America (2009), 73, 90, 141, 165
  One Simple Idea (2016) / formerly *The Empire of Mind*, 17–19
  as police reporter, 132, 167
  Practical Magick (2025), 75, 166
  Doc Savage and, 17–18
  The Unbelievable with Dan Aykroyd (History Channel) and, 69–70
Howe, Irving, *The American Newness*, 102
Hoyt, Palmer, 132–133
Hubbard, L. Ron, *Dianetics*, 39
Human Personality and Its Survival of Bodily Death (Myers), 51–52, 59
Hume, David, 116, 185
Hurricane Sandy (2012), 91
Hyde, Josh, 164
Hyman, Ray, 30–31, 176–177, 190–192
hypnagogia, 75, 162, 189–193, 206
  ganzfeld experiments and, 30–31, 188, 190–193, 203
  nature of, 25, 29–30
hypnopompia, 25, 189–190

hypnotism, 180
  Émile Coué and, 23
  Nancy School of, 23

I

I Ching, 101
Infinite Intelligence (Hill), 14–15, 52, 157–158, 160–161
In Search of the Miraculous (Ouspensky), 78
Institute of Noetic Sciences (IONS), 103, 176–177, 182, 186
insults, as predatory behavior, 85
It Works (R. H. J.), 31–32

J

James, William, 15–16
  Society for Psychical Research (SPR) and, 179–180
  The Varieties of Religious Experience, 207–208
Jarrett, Roy Herbert (R. H. J.), 31–33
  It Works (R. H. J. / Roy Herbert Jarrett), 31–32
Jones, Ernest, 180–181, 199
Journal of Near-Death Studies, 188
Journal of Parapsychology, 190–191
Jowett, Benjamin, 48
Jung, Carl, 126
  Synchronicity, 17
justice, 112–113

K

Kabbalah, 48
Kaczynski, Richard, *Mind Over Magick*, 106–107
Kam-Hansen, Slavenka, 27n
Kaptchuk, Ted J., 28
karma, 113
Kaufmann, Walter, 113
Kekecs, Zoltan, 122
Khan, Hazrat Inayat, 62–63
Khan, Noor Inayat, 63
Kia (Spare), 44–45
Kidman, Nicole, 65
King, Stephen, 126
Kripalmy, Jeffrey J., *Authors of the Impossible*, 59
Krishnamurti, Jiddu, 26–27
  Think on These Things, 72–74
The Kybalion (2022 documentary), 69

L

Labouré, Catherine, 46
Langer, Ellen, 166–167
Lasch, Christopher, 64
LaVey, Anton, 167
  Erotic Crystallization Inertia (ECI), 65
  total environment and, 128
The Law of Success (Hill), 76, 153
Lennon, John, 27
Lévi, Eliphas (Alphonse-Louis Constant), 44–47
  astral light and, 44–46
  on Baphomet, 47
  Doctrine and Ritual of High Magic, 45, 75–76
  on Universal Religion, 46–47
Lewis, C. S., *Mere Christianity*, 38
Liberace, 143–144
Liébeault, Ambroise-Auguste, 23
love, hate and, 112
Lucifer / Lucifuge (Waite), 46

M

"The Magic of Believing" (song), 144
The Magic of Believing (Bristol), 131–133, 136, 139–140, 141–142, 143–147, 149–150, 151
The Magic of Believing for Young People (Bristol), 151
The Magic Story (Dey), 127–128, 129
Maimonides Medical Center, Division of Parapsychology and Psychophysics, 188
"making it." *see* success / "making it"
Maltz, Maxwell, 22, 35–38, 40–41
  as cosmetic surgeon, 36, 38
  Psycho-Cybernetics, 35, 36–41
manifesto, dual self and, 129
mantras / affirmations, 17, 22–27, 28–29, 32, 34–35, 37
The Marriage of Heaven and Hell (Blake), 205–206

The Master Key to Riches (Hill), 81
Master Mind groups, 77, 169
materialism, 183–184, 197, 204–205
Maury, Alfred, 25n
Mavromatis, Andreas, 25n
Mayan Long-Count calendar, 101
McCartney, Paul, 27
McComb, Samuel, *Body, Mind, and Spirit* (with Worcester), 207–209
McDougall, William, 181
meditation, 37–38, 63, 162
mediums, 180. *see also* ESP
Meetings with Remarkable Men (Gurdjieff), 97–99
Mere Christianity (Lewis), 38
Mesmer, Franz Anton, 44, 45
Mikituk, Anthony, 45
mind alchemy, 21–41
  ganzfeld experiments and, 30–31, 188, 190–193, 203
  mantras / affirmations and, 17, 22–27, 28–29, 32, 34–35, 37
  placebo research and, 15, 22, 24, 27–28, 151
  positive-mind tradition and, 31–32, 33
  see also autosuggestion
Mind Over Magick (Kaczynski), 106–107
The Miracle Club (Horowitz), 202
The Miracle of a Definite Chief Aim (Horowitz), 10, 11–13

Miraculous Medal, 46
Monroe, Marilyn, 144
Murphy, Joseph, *Power of Your Subconscious*, 141
Museum of the Moving Image (Astoria, New York), 68
My Animal (2023 film), 69
Myers, Frederic W. H., 25, 189
  Human Personality and Its Survival of Bodily Death, 51–52, 59
  Society for Psychical Research (SPR) and, 179–180
My Method, Including American Impressions (Coué), 32–33

N

"Nancy School" of hypnotism, 23
Napoleon Hill Success Course, 10, 11–15
Needleman, Jacob, 74
Negro World (newspaper), 32
New Age, 60, 142
New Age (journal), 56
New Frontiers of the Mind (Rhine), 16–17, 195
New Thought (mind-power literature), 141, 151, 157–158, 207, 208
New World of the Mind (Rhine), 201
The New Yorker, 60
The New York Times, 9, 64
Nietzsche, Friedrich, *Beyond Good and Evil*, 113
Noah, Daniel, 69

Noory, George, 144
North American Review, 154, 156
Norumbega Tower (Weston, Massachusetts), 67–68
Nous, 52, 157

O

obfuscation, as predatory behavior, 85–86
Occult America (Horowitz), 73, 90, 141, 165
One Simple Idea (Horowitz), 17–19
On Will in Nature (Schopenhauer), 45
Orage, A. R., *Psychological Exercises and Essays* (formerly *The Active Mind*), 56–58
orgone, 52
Ouspensky, P. D., *In Search of the Miraculous*, 78
Oxford Group, 28

P

The Pall Mall Gazette, 154
parapsychology, 9–13, 179–206
  Daryl J. Bem and, 102–107, 108, 122–123, 148, 194–196
  challenges for, 199–206
  data reporting and, 194–196
  Duke University Parapsychology Laboratory / Rhine Research Center and, 9, 11–13, 16–17, 147–148, 181–187, 188–189, 200–202
  Extraordinary Evidence: ESP Is Real (podcast), 69
  as formal academic science, 10–11, 179–180
  Charles Honorton and, 30, 185, 188–193
  Ray Hyman and, 30–31, 176–177, 190–192
  hypnagogia and, 25, 29–31, 75, 162, 188–193, 203, 206
  hypnopompia and, 25, 189–190
  Carl Jung and, 17
  Maimonides Medical Center, Division of Parapsychology and Psychophysics, 188
  misreporting in, 194–196
  passion and, 17, 38, 48, 59, 195
  Dean Radin and, 103, 176–178, 182, 186, 193, 194
  relative funding for research, 193–194
  Seven Laws of Parapsychology, 206
  Zener card tests and, 11–12, 16, 180, 184, 186, 187, 190
  see also ESP
Peale, Norman Vincent, *The Positive Principle Today*, 144–145
Penguin Random House, 35–36, 45, 60, 76, 165
pentagram, 47, 67
Perry, Jim, 69
perseverance, 97–124
  Daryl J. Bem and, 102–107, 122–123

perseverance (*cont.*)
  entropy and, 114, 117–118
  Neville Goddard and, 110–113, 116–121
  G. I. Gurdjieff and, 97–99
  hindsight and, 99–102
  retrocausality and, 102–113, 121
  R. A. Schwaller de Lubicz on cycles and, 100–102
philanthropy, 156
placebo research, 15, 22, 24, 27–28, 151
Planck, Max, 205
Plato, *Symposium*, 48
Poe, Edgar Allan, 126
positive-mind tradition, 31–32, 33
The Positive Principle Today (Peale), 144–145
positron, 118–119
Power (Emerson), 137–138
Power of Your Subconscious (Murphy), 141
Powers, Melvin, 39
Prabhupada, Swami, 94
Practical Magick (Horowitz), 75, 166
precognition, 59, 102–106, 121–122, 148, 151, 182, 186–187, 194–196, 202, 203
predatory personalities, 81–95
  aftereffect of predatory behavior, 83–84
  being seen and, 93–95
  cognitive and emotional sophistication of, 83–84
  Frederick Douglass and, 88–90, 91, 93
  nature of, 81–82
  parasitical *vs.* creative variant, 82–83
  separating from, 87–88, 91–93
  varieties of predatory experience, 85–87
Prentice-Hall, 35–36, 39, 151
Princeton University, 147–148
Project Stargate, 10, 62, 173–178, 193
Prometheus (2012 film), 128–129
The Proof Is Out There (History Channel show), 70
psi phenomena. *see* ESP; parapsychology
psyche
  extraphysical component of, 182–183. *see also* ESP
  nature of, 9
psychics, 60–62, 173–178
Psycho-Cybernetics (Maltz), 35, 36–41
psychokinesis (PK), 147, 182, 186–187, 203
Psychological Exercises and Essays (formerly *The Active Mind*, Orage), 56–58
Psychology, Religion, and Healing (Weatherhead), 29, 40–41
purpose, dual self and, 129–130
putdowns, as predatory behavior, 85
Putin, Vladimir, 176
Pyron, Darden Asbury, 143

Q

quantum computing, 108
  Willow (quantum-computing processor), 13–14, 204–205
quantum physics / mechanics, 10, 14n, 114–116, 147, 203, 206

R

Radin, Dean, 103, 176–178, 182, 186, 193, 194
Randi, James, 62, 102
Random House, 68
Reagan, Nancy, 35
Reich, Wilhelm, 52
reincarnation, 188
remote viewing (RV), 9–11, 180, 187–188
  Project Stargate, 10, 62, 173–178, 193
respectability, 26
retrocausality, 102–116, 182, 186–187, 201, 206
  nature of, 102–107
  perseverance and, 102–113, 121
  potential uses of, 107–116
reversals, as predatory behavior, 86
Rhine, J. B., 9–13, 60, 81, 174
  Duke University Parapsychology Laboratory, 9, 11–13, 16–17, 147–148, 181–182, 184–187, 188–189, 200–202
  Extrasensory Perception, 16, 186

New Frontiers of the Mind, 16–17, 195
New World of the Mind, 201
  Dean Radin as successor to, 176–178
Rhine, Louisa, 181
Richet, Charles, 180
Robbins, Anthony, 22
Rockefeller Foundation, 12
Royal Society Open Science, 122

S

Savage, Doc, 17–18
Schopenhauer, Arthur, *On Will in Nature*, 45
Schouten, Sybo, 177, 193
Schrödinger, Erwin, 103, 111, 116
Schwaller de Lubicz, R. A., 100–102
Schwarzenegger, Arnold, 144
self-honesty, 64–65, 71–74, 150
self-image, 21–25, 35–38
Self Mastery Through Conscious Autosuggestion (Coué), 23–24, 34–35
self-programming, mantras / affirmations in, 17, 22–27, 28–29, 32, 34–35
self-suggestion. *see* autosuggestion
sensory deprivation, 30, 189–190, 206
Seven Laws of Parapsychology, 206

sex transmutation
  being gay and, 48, 49
  creative expression and, 50, 51–52, 53
  Napoleon Hill and, 43–44, 47–53
  impacts and applications of, 50–53
  recap, 53
Sheehan, Daniel, 115–116
sheep-goat effects, 15
Sheldrake, Rupert, 187, 197, 201–202
sigils, 47, 150
silence, 75–77
Simon & Schuster, 58
sixth sense
  "astral light" and, 44–47
  basics of, 47–50
  Napoleon Hill and, 14–15, 43–44, 47–53
  mentalism and, 9
  Willow (quantum-computing processor) and, 13–14, 204–205
  see also ESP; parapsychology
Society for Psychical Research (SPR), 177, 179–180, 193
Spare, Austin Osman, 44–45
  Formulae of Zos Vel Thanatos, 60
speaking, dual self and, 129
SpectreVision, 69
Spencer, Herbert, 154–155
Spiritualism, 181
Stargate, 10, 62, 173–178, 193
Steele, Scorpio, 17–19
Stevenson, Ian, 188
Stevenson, Robert Louis, 126
Stone, W. Clement, 12
string theory, 201–203
success / "making it," 131–151
  acquisitiveness, 44, 166
  The Magic of Believing (Bristol), 131–133, 136, 139–140, 141–142, 143–147, 149–150, 151
  timelines and, 141–142, 165–168
Sufism, 62–63
Swedenborg, Emanuel, 157
Symposium (Plato), 48
Synchronicity (Jung), 17

T

Tantra, 48
Taoism, 48, 101
Tao Te Ching, 101
Tarot, 47, 63–64
Taylor, Bob, 153–154
telepathy, 9–10, 59, 179–181, 186–188, 199
  ganzfeld experiments, 30–31, 188, 190–193, 203
  see also ESP
Theosophy, 26–27
Think and Grow Rich (Hill), 9, 14–15, 16, 21, 39–40, 43, 48–49, 59, 68, 126–127, 153, 169–171
Think on These Things (Krishnamurti), 72–74
30-Day Mental Challenge, 107–110, 207–209

Thomas, Ronni, 69
Thomas Nelson & Sons, 39
Three Magic Words (formerly *The Key to Power and Personal Peace*, Andersen), 39
titles, of books, 40
T.N.T. (Bristol), 134–139, 151
Tolstoy, Leo, *War and Peace*, 100
Transcendental Magic (Waite), 45–46
Transcendental Meditation (TM), 37–38
Trine, Ralph Waldo, 155
Troward, Thomas, 158–159, 164
True Will (Crowley), 44
Trussell, Duncan, 50
Tupolev planes, 174–176, 178

U

Ukraine, 173, 174, 176
The Unbelievable with Dan Aykroyd (History Channel show), 69–70
undelivered gifts or promises, as predatory behavior, 86
Universal Religion, 46–47
University of Chicago, 181
University of Oregon, 176n, 190–191
University of San Diego (USD), "Quantum Retrocausation" conference, 114–116
University of Virginia, Division of Perceptual Studies, 188
University of West Virginia, 181
Utts, Jessica, 176, 177, 191, 193

V

Vanden Broeck, André, *Al-Kemi*, 101–102
The Varieties of Religious Experience (James), 207–208
Vedic theology, 26–27, 113
Vilayat, Pir, 63
visualization, 37, 65, 136–137, 157, 159, 161–163
Vril: The Power of the Coming Race (Bulwer-Lytton), 44

W

Waite, Arthur Edward, *Transcendental Magic*, 45–46
The Wall Street Journal, 174
War and Peace (Tolstoy), 100
Warcollier, René, 180
Wattles, Wallace D., 155
Wealth (Emerson), 137, 138–139
Weatherhead, Leslie D., 28–29
Psychology, Religion, and Healing, 29, 40–41
Weaver, Warren, 12, 185, 200–202
Weiler, Craig, 197–198
Wiener, Norbert, 36
Wikipedia, 63, 174, 186, 193, 197
Wild Talents (Fort), 179
Willow (quantum-computing processor), 13–14, 204–205
Wilshire Book Company, 39
Wilson, Brian, 35
wish, power of single, 55–80
author experiences with, 58–59, 60, 67–70, 73, 76–77
clarity of intent and, 66–71, 74

wish, power of single (*cont.*)
   deciding what you want, 56–58
   Definite Chief Aim (DCA) and, 10, 11–13, 69, 70–71, 97, 129–130
   letter to an inmate, 77–80
   A. R. Orage and, 56–58
   psychics and, 60–62
   self-honesty and, 64–65, 71–74, 150
   silence and, 75–77
   Sufism and, 62–63
   Tarot and, 63–64
   wishcraft technique and, 74–75

Wood, Elijah, 69
Worcester, Elwood, *Body, Mind, and Spirit* (with McComb), 207–209

Y

Your Invisible Power (Behrend), 158–159

Z

Zener, Karl E., 184
Zener cards, 11–12, 16, 180, 184, 186, 187, 190

About the Author

MITCH HOROWITZ is a historian of alternative spirituality and one of today's most literate voices of esoterica, mysticism, and parapsychology. Mitch is the PEN Award-winning author of books including *Occult America, One Simple Idea, The Miracle Club, Daydream Believer, Uncertain Places, Modern Occultism, Happy Warriors,* and *Practical Magick.* The *Washington Post* says Mitch

Jacqueline Castel

"treats esoteric ideas and movements with an even-handed intellectual studiousness that is too often lost in today's raised-voice discussions." *Filmmaker Magazine* calls him "a genius at distilling down esoteric concepts." Mitch hosts Discovery / HBO Max's *Alien Encounters: Fact or Fiction,* SpectreVision's podcast, *Extraordinary Evidence: ESP Is Real,* and plays himself in AMC-

Shudder's *V/H/S/BEYOND*, a Critics Choice Award nominee for best movie made for television. He appears regularly on the History Channel's *The Unbelievable with Dan Aykroyd*, among other shows. A former vice president at Penguin Random House, Mitch has written on alternative spirituality for *The New York Times, The Wall Street Journal, The Washington Post, Time, Politico,* and appeared widely in national media. Mitch's writing has called attention to the worldwide problem of violence against accused witches, helping draw notice to the human-rights element of the issue. Mitch's work is translated into languages including French, German, Arabic, Hebrew, Chinese, Italian, Spanish, Korean, Japanese, and Portuguese. His book *Awakened Mind* is the first work of New Thought translated and published in Saudi Arabia. He is censored in China.

www.ingramcontent.com/pod-product-compliance
Lightning Source LLC
Chambersburg PA
CBHW071959070526
44583CB00015B/1263